BY WHAT
AUTHORITY?

By What Authority?

The Open Synod Group Report on Authority in The Church of England

Edited by
Robert Jeffery

MOWBRAY
LONDON & OXFORD

First published 1987
by A. R. Mowbray & Co. Ltd,
Saint Thomas House, Becket Street,
Oxford, OX1 1SJ

British Library Cataloguing in Publication Data:

By what authority.
　1. Church of England 2. Church —
　Authority
　I. Jeffery, Robert
　262'.8　　　　　BX5131.2

ISBN 0-264-67139-2

The Open Synod Group:

Membership of the Open Synod Group is available to all who are concerned about the issues raised in this book. It is not limited to members of the General Synod and groups of members are developing in many Dioceses.

For further details contact the Secretary:

Mrs Terry Garley,
64 Wyndale Drive,
Kirk Hallam,
Ilkeston,
DE7 4JG.

Note on Contributors.

Stephen Sykes is Regius Professor of Divinity in the University of Cambridge.

Ruth Etchells is Principal of Cranmer Hall with St John's College, Durham (until April 1988).

Peter Baelz, Dean of Durham, was formerly Professor of Moral and Pastoral Theology in the University of Oxford.

Adrian Hastings is Professor of Theology in the University of Leeds.

Robert Jeffery who introduces and sums up the proceedings is Dean of Worcester.

Contents

Foreword: The Revd. Michael O'Connor,
Chairman of the Open Synod Group   xi

1 Setting the Scene
            Robert Jeffery   1

2 Authority in the Church of England
            Stephen Sykes   7

3 The Authority of the Bible
            Ruth Etchells   26

4 The Authority of Reason and Conscience
            Peter Baelz   42

5 The Authority of the Church, Universal and
  Local
            Adrian Hastings   51

6 An Agenda for the Church?
            Robert Jeffery   65

  Postscript: Cleansing the Temple: A Sermon by
  Stephen Sykes   77

Foreword

Michael O'Connor

With the media actively discussing the imminent prospect of schism, whether as the result of disagreements over doctrine or the prospect of the Ordination of Women to the Priesthood, it is clear that while ferment is recognized to be a continuing state for the Church something more traumatic is taking place in the Church of England at the moment. It is also clear that behind the particular issues there lies a more fundamental disagreement about the nature of the different authorities of Scripture, Tradition, Reason and Conscience, and what weight should be given to each of these when they appear to conflict. Because Christians differ about these basic questions it is not to be wondered at that they not only differ also on consequential issues, but that they also find it difficult to discuss their differences.

In such a situation those who care for the continuing life of the Church have a dual responsibility, first to think through and articulate where they stand themselves, and secondly to seek opportunities to listen to and share with others who hold differing views. The Open Synod Group, which both represents the liberal tradition in the Church and also exists as a forum where those with a variety of outlooks can meet together, has a particular responsibility in this area, and the Group's Conference at High Leigh in February 1987 was an attempt, and those who took part felt that it was a significant attempt, to do just this.

The Group owes a debt of gratitude to our four Speakers who were willing not only to offer us their particular contributions, but also to share in the life of the Conference and to respond to the contributions of others taking part. Secondly the Conference acquired its significance because so many other Groups and Societies across the whole theological spectrum responded to our invitation to send representatives to share in our discussions, and that they did so to great effect.

Finally, it is surely notable that it was the universal view of those who took part that it was our worship together which provided the key to the whole.

We offer this Report of our Conference to the Church in the hope that it may be of value in that continuing discussion at all levels in the Church which High Leigh showed to be not simply possible but indeed the only way forward.

1

Setting The Scene

Robert Jeffery

'There is a Cancer in the Church of England' cried the
Revd David Holloway as he pointed to what he saw as a
lack of faithfulness by some Bishops to the true preaching
of the Gospel. The General Synod, as elected in 1985,
has seemed to some of its members, old and new, to be in
something of a state of confusion. Feelings seem to be
running high and there is around a sense of bewilderment
about where the Church is going. There is, of course, a
proper sense in which the Church reflects the Age in
which it lives. Politically, our Society has undergone a
shift to the right and with a strong emphasis on the
personal. There has been an affirmation of monetarism
allied to the politics of certainty. Some of this spirit is
permeating the Church, though the Church has been
more resistant than some other aspects of Society.

There are other forces at work as well. Adrian Hastings
in his very important book *The History of English Christianity 1920–85* points out that the General Synod is still
grappling with the dying causes of the 1960s and at some
points they do not fit today's world. Alan Wilkinson has
argued in *The Church of England and the First World War*
that the Church is still trying to come to terms with the
Agenda created by the deep traumas of that war. It is
small wonder that there are uncertainties and confusions.
At the same time, as the speakers at the Conference
reminded us, this is no new thing. There has never been a
time when the Church has avoided turmoil of some sort.
Indeed compared with earlier Ages our situation is rather
mild, though the impact of secularization has probably

never been so strong. The language of 'Cancer' is too emotive. What we began to see was that conflict, crisis and turmoil can be used positively to bring new life.

Anyone who looks at the Church of England since 1945 will see a series of areas where agreement has been very difficult, if not impossible, to achieve. The rows over the establishment of the Church of South India, the many abortive Church Union Schemes, the failure to agree a pattern for Evangelism, the inability to really face the questions of theological education and the uncertainties over the deployment of clergy manpower, have all to be noted. Yet there have been achievements and growing understanding between differing views within the Church. The revision of Canon Law, the production of the Alternative Service Book, the flexibility brought about by the Pastoral Measure are all very welcome. We should also note a growing consensus on ethical and social issues which the Church has achieved.

The present unrest in the Church springs partly from the 'Spirit of the Age' and also from two other factors: the failure of the Covenanting for Unity Proposals to achieve a sufficient majority and the growing pressure for the Ordination of Women to the Priesthood in the Church of England. Alongside this there has been a considerable growth in strength and confidence within the Evangelical wing of the Church of England. There is also the steady influence of the Charismatic Movement, now well documented in Josephine Bax's book *The Good Wine*. For at least 15 years people have been concerned about the growing gap between academic theology and the parishes and parish clergy. This revealed itself fully in public in what has become known as 'The Durham Affair' when a leading academic became Bishop and expressed views which many felt threatened the foundations of Faith.

The last three years have seen these tendencies affecting the way the General Synod has operated, very much in the eye of the mass media and a fairly unsympathetic popular Press. What many have observed in the Church has been a muddle, with Bishops under pressure and a Church unable to make firm decisions. Thus, the General Synod in relation to the Remarriage of Divorced people has left every Vicar to their own devices. Faced with an increasing number of Women Priests in the Anglican Communion, the Church of England will not allow them to minister in this country, even on a limited basis. The way in which the Church has moved very slowly over the matter of the Ordination of Women to the Priesthood (even though in 1975 it declared that there were no theological objections to it) has bewildered many. The Durham Affair simmers on and the House of Bishops has been forced to issue statements which in the end please hardly anybody. At the heart of this lies the development of Synodical Government, still fairly new, which has profoundly affected the way in which Bishops are able to operate inside the Church. The Bishop of Southwark recently commented that while people look to the Bishops for authority, their own decision-making has a representative and constitutional character. He continued:

> Our jurisdiction is therefore subject to Canons and decisions of the whole Church, which include quite specific safeguards like the freehold that most incumbents enjoy.
>
> . . . One of the difficulties of being an Anglican Bishop is that respect for the teaching authority of the Bishop is conditioned – inevitably – by the historic division between reformed and catholic.

He then pointed out that one of the virtues of the present situation is that the House of Bishops has been forced to act and to think corporately in a way in which they had not often done before.

Against this background the Open Synod Group held its Conference at High Leigh at the end of January 1987. The Open Synod Group is a strange body. Its origins lie in what used to be called the 'Non-Party Group' in the old Church Assembly. This was a group of Laity who did not wish to be aligned to the Catholic or Evangelical groups in the Assembly. Thus while both groups developed a 'Party Line' the middle ground was much more disparate, yet needed to share, understand and support each other. With the development of Synodical Government, the 'Non-Party Group' became the NEW SYNOD GROUP. They saw their function as trying to help the members of the Church to understand Synodical Government and take an informed part within it. There was also a concern to try to see that the middle ground of the Church was represented. This group subsequently became the 'Open Synod Group'. It claims to have no 'Party Line' but to be there to enable discussion and provide information for people to consider the issues coming before the Synod. Inevitably, however, as the Church has become more polarized, the Open Synod Group has been forced to express what it really stands for. Just because the Open Synod Group stands in the centre it would be very easy for it to become a 'soft centre'. It has, however, sought to stand for openness, rather than for fixed views. It has generally supported change rather than the *status quo*. It has been accused of being woolly, lacking in spirituality and expressing old-fashioned, liberal views.

The 1987 Conference was described as 'an exercise in reconciliation'. It was organized so that people of differing views and groups within the Church of England might meet together to consider a common problem – Authority in the Church. It is an issue which underlines many of the current problems in the Church, but is not, in itself, a party issue. The Conference was fully booked. There were present representatives of the Evangelical and Catholic groupings as well as members of the Movement for the Ordination of Women and the Gay Christian Movement. There was a small group of Officers from Church House and not a few Deans and Archdeacons. There was a good mix of women and men, though it was acknowledged that the membership was somewhat middle-class and middle-aged. There were some old hands, like Dame Christian Howard, now retired from the General Synod but there were also many who were either new members of the General Synod or people who are genuinely concerned about what is happening to the Church at the present time. We all came to participate, to share and to learn.

The Conference began with a major Paper from Professor Sykes, who has written and thought much about the subject of Authority in Anglicanism. This was followed by responses to his Paper looking at the area of Scripture, Reason and the Church from three other leading theologians. Groups were held to assimilate and expand on the material. There was a 'Question Time' Session and an opportunity for further comment at the end of the Conference. Professor Sykes in his book *The Identity of Christianity* has argued that the proper arena for reconciliation of doctrinal differences lies within the context of Worship and Prayer. This was very much what happened in the Conference. The Worship took the form of formal services and prayers and a long extended Eucharist on the last morning to which all the groups contributed by means of prayer, readings, drama, mime and meditation.

This Report is written in the hope that others who read it may enter into some of the thinking and share the insights which emerged. There follows the Papers delivered at the Conference and in a final Chapter we shall see how the Conference responded and what it may mean for us.

2

Authority in The Church of England

Stephen Sykes

First, I asked myself why there should be such public concern about *this* particular issue at *this* particular time. The reason, as ever, seems to be the conjunction of a variety of pressures and problems, not just one pressure.

For example, it is a feature of our times that the 20-year old revolution carried out in the Church of Rome following the Second Vatican Council has seriously disturbed the world Christian ecology. By using that image I mean to imply the interdependence of Christian denominations. Anglicans, for example, derive support and sustenance for what they are as Anglicans at least in part from what Roman Catholics are on the one hand, and from what Baptists are, on the other. But if it is true, as Avery Dulles has recently argued in his book, *Catholicity*, that the Roman Catholic Church has internalized no less than ten standard Protestant criticisms of Catholicism, then the ecological balance is altered, and the question arises whether the separations out of which the Protestant movements arose are any longer necessary. All the major European reformers characterized their protest movements as provisional and regrettable necessities, and longed for a time when they would cease to be so. The question is, whether that time has now come?

Another reason for public concern about Anglican authority has to do with the security of one of its favourite appeals, the 'fundamental articles' apologia. From the 16th century onwards Anglicans have insisted that the theological basis of the Anglican Church is nothing less, and nothing more, than the faith of the primitive church, summed up in the Catholic creeds and expressed in various ways in the writings of the early Greek and Latin fathers. Since the 19th century there have been dissident Anglicans, like John Henry Newman, who thought that there could not be so *few* elements in Christian faith as that, or those who, like Hastings Rashdall, saw no reason why there should be so *many*. The theory of development may force Anglicans inclined to Newman's views to ask questions about Mariology and Papal Infallibility, and on the other the phenomenon of biblical criticism may prompt liberals to question the Virgin Birth and the Bodily Resurrection. In either case what is being scrutinized is the theory of fundamentals in which Anglicans have invested over 400 years of apologetic effort, but which is neither as simple as it sounds, nor as intellectually unchallengeable as is sometimes assumed.

Finally, the Church of England has a new mode of government. The General Synod, far from having had a period during which it could, so to speak, bed itself down, has been forced to debate and in some cases to decide a series of highly charged and complex problems, such as liturgical revision, matters of social and political ethics, schemes of ecumenical co-operation, and agreed statements on doctrinal issues. Changes in its relationship with Parliament have greatly complicated an already difficult period of adjustment. Despite this constitutional tie of most doubtful value, leading members of the Church of England who have been so swift to complain about the inadequacies of the Synod of Westminster, ought surely to have had the humility to consider the more than 100 years' experience of synodical government which Anglicans in other parts of the world have had, for example in the USA, New Zealand, Ireland and South Africa. Be that as it may, the coincidence of pressures to make decisions and the comparative novelty of the procedures have certainly contributed to the special anxiety which attends the present moment.

But I have to say also that the rhetoric of crisis and of imminent catastrophe which one may now hear tends to deflect attention from a deeper and broader question. Here it is important to affirm that the theological issue we must address in this Conference is nothing less than *authority in the Church of Christ herself.*

Anglicans understand themselves, in the words of Canon A.1., to 'belong to the true and apostolic Church of Christ'. And it is in virtue of our membership of *that* Church that we must ask the question, whether there has ever been a time when conflict has not characterized her life, and whether such conflicts have not always raised the question of final authority. It is something of a temptation to imagine that in other centuries and in other countries things were otherwise. But the books of the New Testament themselves would not have been written had there been peace in even the apostolic age.

Although contemporary New Testament criticism has sharpened our awareness of the complexity and diversity of the dissentions and schisms of the primitive communities, it is an extremely Anglican thing to do to point out the history of dispute. The first major *Apology of the Church of England*, published by Bishop Jewel of Salisbury in 1562, contains a long passage recounting the history of internal conflict starting with the Church in Corinth in the days of St. Paul, and continuing into the late medieval times. Jewel cites *en route* the fifth century Christian historian, Socrates, who remarked that Christians 'for their dissentions and sundry sects . . . were laughed and jested at openly of the people in their stages and common game plays'. Not that Jewel thought this a desirable state for the Church to be in:

> Of a truth, unity and concord doth best become
> religion, yet is not unity the sure and certain mark
> whereby to know the Church of God.
> (*Apology*, Part III, ed. J. E. Booty, Charlottesville,
> 1963, p.47)

The chronic recurrence of conflict in Christianity
reinforces the suspicion that criteria for making decisions
in the Church are not in themselves simple. So the issue
of authority in the Church of Christ is not merely a
matter of evolving a decision-making procedure which is
final and unequivocal, as though the criteria for making
decisions were already beyond dispute. Disputes of any
seriousness and complexity are almost invariably also
disputes about the criteria for settlement.

For example, Martin Luther's challenge to theological
debate on the issue of the sale of indulgences was not in
the first instance an attack on the authority of the Papacy.
But it became such an issue, an issue of authority, when
his opponents chose to deny that he had the right to
argue theologically against what the Pope had already put
into effect. From then on the dispute was *both* about the
nature of Christian repentance *and* about authority in the
Church, criteria and structures. Similarly in our own day
there are many disputes which are *both* about theological
issues *and* about criteria and structures. These are normal
Christian disputes, and the rhetoric of crisis does us a
disservice in deflecting our attention from the nature of
Christian history. Those who sometimes speak as though
reconciliation with the Papacy would be the only way of
resolving the Anglican 'crisis of authority' forget that
the criteria of authority are not locked up in the breast of
one man. The growing capacity of Roman Catholic
bishops and theologians openly to discuss matters which
the Pope has purported to decide, such as the question of
the control of conception, the marriage of priests, the

ordination of women to the priesthood, and the treatment of practising homosexuals and of divorcees – this reminds us that there is an important function in controversy which is related to the whole course of Christian history and to the very embodiment of the Church of Christ in time.

But the strength and validity of a view of this kind will only become apparent if we examine with greater patience some fundamental aspects of the theology of authority.

1 *God, the single divine source of all authority, takes the pathway among humanity of challengeability and service*

Anglicans are accustomed, through their use of the Psalter, to 'ascribe power unto the Lord' (Psalm 29.2). But what kind of power? The very term 'Lord of hosts' passes, in the biblical period, through a series of changes of meaning, which continued in translations into the Greek *kurios pantocrator* (Lord almighty) and into the Latin *deus omnipotens*. Careless use of the idea of omnipotence conceals the fact that, in the Old Testament, the power of God is not of the kind which obliterates the opposition by mere fiat. Rather, it is the sort of power which helps Israel in its confrontations, and which therefore has to admit the reality and strength of the opposition. From the start, then, the power of God is challengeable. The spiritual importance of this thought is apparent in the writings of both Jeremiah and Job. The relationship with God depicted in these works in one which permits a moment of controversy with God from within the heart of suffering and perplexity.

This view of the power of God is more strongly reinforced within the New Testament. For Jesus Christ takes with humanity the pathway of humility, of service and of weakness, as his route to the victory of the Cross.

Here again is no obliteration of the powers of evil by mere fiat, but a patient persistence with the reality and strength of the opposition which is routed at the very moment of maximum helplessness.

The process of transformation of the very notion of divine power which this history entails is confirmed by the record of Jesus' explicit teaching on the nature of authority, when he denies the relevance of the example of dominative authority available in contemporary society: 'It shall not be so among you' (Luke 22.26). He commends, rather, the role and humility of a servant. Note, if you will, that Jesus does not deny the fact that authority in the community will require the exercise of power. But, he seems to imply, the responsibilities of the great and of leaders, when exercised in the manner of a servant, will inevitably involve suffering, here and now. The pathway of service, the route of challengeability, will be one of pain and of cost. The avoidance of pain, a human instinct of great profundity, is surely one of the motives guiding the Church's retreat from service in its exercise of authority, and the cause of its repeated and regrettable tendency to clothe itself in the mantle of unchallengeability.

2   *God gives his gifts to the whole Church*

One of the major reasons why service must characterize the Christian exercise of leadership is the fact that God has given gifts to the *whole* church. His gifts are his empowerment of the body for its task of being the church in the world. The Gospel is 'the power of God unto salvation, to everyone that believeth' (Romans 1.16). But this gospel is, precisely, the gospel of the crucified and risen Lord. It is the whole church, and 'every member of the same in his vocation and ministry', which engages in the apostolic mission of 'declaring the wonderful deeds of him who called (us) out of darkness into his marvellous light' (I Peter 2.9). Leadership in the Church is always leadership in her mission, in her realization of her fundamental identity as the people of God, and necessarily involves attention to the particularity of the Holy Spirit's work in each one.

If every Christian has his or her own special 'vocation and ministry', then the authority which belongs to the act of proclaiming the Gospel of Christ inheres in each and every Christian person. There is a proper sovereignty which belongs to every member of God's own people which constitutes them corporately, as a *royal* priesthood. Christians share eschatologically in the victory of Christ, a victory over the world, the flesh and the devil in which they participate in virtue of their baptism.

Giving the whole people of God access to the Scriptures through the interpretative medium of the liturgy was the fundamental catechetical act of empowering the people, taken in the 16th century. It was the reformers' conviction that knowledge of the Scriptures was a necessary resource for the mission of the whole Church. The Christian life was such that an uninstructed or passive laity was unthinkable. And although Cranmer acknowledged that Scripture contained complexities, nonetheless he believed that its fundamental message was not too difficult even for the illiterate:

> For God receiveth the learned and the unlearned, and casteth away none, but is indifferent to all. All the scripture is full, as well of low valleys, plainways, and easy for men to use and walk in; as also of high hills and mountains, which few men can climb into.
>
> (Second Homily, 'To the Reading and Knowledge of Holy Scriptures', *The Book of Homilies*.)

And for the controversial times in which he lived, it was essential that the whole Church be sufficiently instructed to be able to discriminate between the claims of rival authorities, theological and ecclesiastical.

Here is a fundamental feature of the Anglican tradition which is anything but a matter of antiquarian interest. It involves the notion of a distribution of authority, which has received repeated endorsement to our own century. At the Lambeth Conference of 1948, a Committee of Bishops sought to epitomize this dispersal of authority in the following way:

> Authority, as inherited by the Anglican Communion from the undivided Church of the early centuries of the Christian era, is single in that it is derived from a single Divine source, and reflects within itself the richness and historicity of the Divine Revelation, the authority of the eternal Father, the incarnate Son, and the life-giving Spirit. It is distributed among Scripture, Tradition, Creeds, the Ministry of the Word and Sacraments, the witness of saints, and the *consensus fidelium*, which is the continuing experience of the Holy Spirit through His faithful people in the Church. It is thus a dispersed rather than a centralized authority having many elements which combine, interact with, and check each other; these elements together contributing by a process of mutual support, mutual checking, and redressing of errors or exaggerations to the many-sided fullness of the authority which Christ has committed to His Church. Where this authority of Christ is to be found mediated not in one mode but in several we recognize in this multiplicity God's loving provision against the temptations to tyranny and the dangers of unchecked power.

It is important to make two things clear about the theory of this now celebrated document. It would be erroneous to conclude from the phrase 'a dispersed rather than a centralized authority' that it has no conception of how the Church as a whole could proceed to make coherent decisions. On the contrary, it contains in the passage which follows a very strong affirmation of the episcopate, 'in synodical association with (the) clergy and laity', as the 'source and centre' of our order. Provinces, the normal decision-making unit in the Anglican Communion, contain, of course, many bishops, and provincial synods necessarily constitute a manifestation of centralized authority. By analogy, then, there would be nothing incongruous, on the basis of this common Anglican experience, in an international or universal decision-making body, provided it, too, reflected the 'synodical association' spoken of.

Secondly, the theology of authority which the document is striving to express does not constitute simply an Anglican theory, a rationalization of existing differences over against 'papal tyranny' on the one hand, and 'mere congregationalism' on the other. Unless I am very much mistaken, this is the only kind of authority justifiable in the universal Church of Christ, and is one which we as Anglicans have every reason to explore, to expound and to defend, without a hint of that curiously smug self-deprecation which has so paralysed us in our public theological stances of late. Its essential feature is the recognition of the richness and historicity of the divine revelation. The distribution of God's gifts to the whole Church means that there are *voices* of authority, not one unambiguous, unequivocal *voice* of authority. It means that these voices of authority are the consequence of the call of God to every Christian believer to embody the saving Gospel in his or her own life, and to receive the empowering gift of his Holy Spirit to that end.

3 *God calls a special Ministry in his Church, whose limited powers are to be openly acknowledged*

A special ministry entails the act of choosing particular people to exercise leadership or oversight. But these most ambiguous of words conceal a nest of difficulties and potential tensions. There are, after all, different kinds of leadership. The worship of the Church needs to be 'led'; so too does its necessary making of decisions. And one of the potential dangers for the Church is the development of incoherence between the oversight of an ordained ministry, and how it distributes its powers as an organization. The office of the bishop has been traditionally and for very good reason the focus for these differing functions.

The growing size and complexity of the early Church imposed, as one would expect, certain sociological constraints upon it as an organization. We can already see from the New Testament epistles the dangers which attended the development of a special ministry. In the First Epistle of Peter, the author warns the *presbyteroi* or elders that shepherding the flock, now a paid occupation, must not be done with thought of financial gain. They are also alerted to the danger of a domineering style of exercising their powers. Thus arises what Professor Kingsley Barrett has called the 'paradox' of the ministry, which he formulates as follows:

> A church that rejects the gifts of leadership will greatly impoverish itself: a church that allows them to develop in a worldly way will destroy itself.
> (*Church, Ministry and Sacraments in the New Testament*. Exeter 1985, 40.)

Preventing the ministry from developing in 'a worldly way' will entail taking with the utmost seriousness Jesus' warning, "But it shall not be so among you". The whole notion of 'styles of leadership' or 'legitimation of authority' is informed by 'worldly' models available in given societies. We see this better in societies not our own, than in our own case. We observe for example, that some African bishops behave remarkably like some African tribal chiefs; or that some North American Bishops behave like chief executives of successful business corporations. Our own bishops, perhaps, are expected to combine the charisma of a TV personality, with the wisdom of a psychoanalyst, and the skills of a chairperson of a charitable trust. If they subsequently develop qualities of superficial charm, phoney omniscience, and a capacity for devious manipulation, we discover that their supposed 'gifts of leadership' have been allowed to develop 'in a worldly way'.

But what is to stop them so developing? All that we have argued for so far suggests that challengeability must be an important attribute of a Christian person who exercises authority. The document accepted by the Primates' Meeting in Washington DC in April 1981 draws out the meaning of episcopé in Anglicanism in the following way:

> In the continuing process of defining the *consensus fidelium*, Anglicans regard criticism and response as an essential element by which Authority is exercised and experienced and as playing a vital part in the work of the Holy Spirit in maintaining the Church in fidelity to the Apostolic Gospel.

Here the statement explicitly accords status to the practice of 'hearing criticism'. It was when this particular feature of the document was described to me by one extremely prelatical bishop as 'a charter for the bloody-minded' that I knew it contained the truth. For it is precisely a characteristic of those who exercise power 'in a worldly way' to attempt to disguise it, and to protect themselves from criticism. In particular, the history of the Church knows the lengths to which authority will go in order to inhibit access to contrary views. The *consensus fidelium* can be prematurely contrived by the burning, banishing or banning of the opposition and their publications. The only way in which a leadership can prevent appeal to the *consensus* amounting to the phoney consultation of opinions already manipulated in advance is by an honest commitment to the education and nurture of the whole Church.

Anglicans, as we know, have committed themselves unequivocally to a hierarchical church order. The advantage of a hierarchy is that everyone knows officially where the power lies, and at whose door criticism should be laid. (All hierarchies develop unofficial power structures, as those familiar with Barchester Close will not need telling, but that is another story.) The problem for hierarchy in the Christian Church is the fact that it is simultaneously the focus of the exercise of power *and* of the dependence of the whole Church upon Jesus Christ, who is the source of her mission and the foundation of her unity. This problem is the source of that notorious difficulty in the phrase 'a centre of unity'. Bishops and their curates are, especially in the eucharistic celebration, 'the visible focus of the deep and all-embracing communion between Christ and the members of his body' (Ministry Section 14 in *Baptism, Eucharist and Ministry*, World Council of Churches, Faith and Order, Paper 111, p.22). But at the same time, they occupy in relation to their communities, positions of authority which are not beyond challenge, if my account is correct. They would have the right to *claim* to speak with authority to their congregations what they conscientiously believe to be in accordance with God's will for the Church and her mission, to minister – that is, necessarily, to interpret – the Word of God in the name of Christ. In doing so they could not be expected to trim their utterances in order to avoid saying anything which would be subject to discussion, or even challenge and contradiction. On the contrary, Cranmer expected his bishops to be in the thick of controversy, teaching and exhorting with wholesome doctrine and withstanding and convincing gainsayers (from *The Consecration of Bishops*). To be both a focus of eucharistic unity and, even if unsought, a cause and focus of controversy, is no easy vocation. But both seem to me proper consequences of a true theology of authority; and if that were to involve the bishop in personal suffering, that consequence too seems to be part of the normal experience of a disciple of Christ and of the expected cost of the embodiment of the Church of Christ in time.

In the final section of this Paper, I want to draw out a few of the implications of this theology of authority for the Church of England as I see it at the present time.

(i)   Whatever structures of decision-making the Church arrives at they will always embody a tension. This tension is between the fact that the criteria for making decisions about the life of the Church are open to all, and the investment of an inequality of power in a few leaders. Structures are variable, evolving and relative to time and place. For the sake of coherence, however, matters of jurisdiction cannot be wholly separated from church order, and for this reason Anglican structures have always found a special position of leadership for the episcopate. At certain times and in certain places bishops have had very considerable power; even so, my point about a necessary tension is still valid. No bishop ought to rule in such a way as to imply that to him alone is vouchsafed insight into the truth; that is the point of presenting him with a Bible, the very same book available to all, read publicly in the vulgar tongue for the sake of the illiterate. No-one may be required, not even on episcopal authority, to believe as an article of faith 'whatsoever is not read therein, nor may be proved thereby' (Article VI).

The distribution of authority which this requirement implies has led Anglicans to develop decision-making structures which embody, or seek to embody, this principle of open access to the criteria. Hence the idea (in Anglican history not a new idea) of bishop-in-synodical-consultation. Clergy and laity too are part of a normal process of decision-making. The difficulty is that precisely the same tension at once arises. Those who are elected to consult synodically with the bishops enjoy an inequality of power. Their jurisdictional position has turned them into hierarchy, perhaps all the more dangerously because their position of inferiority in the hierarchy of orders conceals from them their actual status in the hierarchy of jurisdiction. They enjoy, it might be thought, a disguised power; and of them too it can be true, as of the most prelactical of episcopal hierarchs of past ages, that they can distort and manipulate the access of the whole Church to the criteria.

But the tension is still there, and must be recognized by all who occupy positions of authority. It can be put in the following form:

> The Christian Church is a Spirit-led community of equal brothers and sisters in the Lord; but in order to realize its radical potential in the context of a secular, stratified society it is obliged itself to become stratified.

Internal inequalities of power are only tolerable for the sake of challenge to the all-too-familiar inequalities of society, rich and poor, slave and free, Jew and Gentile, male and female. For those in a position of jurisdictional power to be oblivious of this tension will put in jeopardy the very notion of authority, which we examined.

(ii) All cultures, as we have suggested, offer to the Church models for the organization of her decision-making procedures. Clement of Rome at the end of the first century delightfully and quite uncritically accepted the military chain of command as a norm, because, presumably, of the scriptural analogies between the Christian life and armed struggle. We do what the bishop tells us, he argues, simply because that is how we achieve coherence in fulfilling the battle aims of the Christian Church. In later times the Imperial Court provided further analogies for the Papal curia, and in our own day, parliamentary procedures have shaped the General Synod's mode of life.

But all of these should stand under the scrutiny of the sentence, 'But it shall not be so among you'. The point of such an injunction is not that there is to hand an alternative, divinely-sanctioned blueprint for church government, which can simply be substituted for these models; nor even that all secular models are of equal desirability or appropriateness, provided they are open to a little gentle criticism. Rather *any* decision-making procedure is perceived as being likely to have secular analogies, not least in the minds of those who operate it, and by virtue of their influence is going to be open to abuse. Therefore, *any* decison-making structure must be open to scrutiny, and this ought to be as true of the workings of the Papacy as of the General Synod. There are many subtle corruptions in the exercise of power, and church history shows that no form of organization is immune from them. The danger is all the more acute because of the claim, which the Church must make, that it is governed by the Holy Spirit.

(iii) Churches under pressure characteristically claim too much for their structures, or alternatively simplify the criteria for decision-making. Both of these are classic forms of legitimation. The latter, the acute simplification of criteria, we can see in Calvin's Church of Geneva, which, he bravely announced, would be governed by the Scriptures alone. This was not the case, and events proved that it could not be the case. In due course Calvin conceded that the criterion of a Spirit-inspired Scripture could not be matched beyond dispute by Spirit-inspired interpreters of Scripture, and he acknowledged the need of humanly fallible scholars and councils of church leaders to decide in matters of controversy. This was a church under pressure to explain the source of its authority; and we see the same phenomenon in the beleaguered Papacy of the 19th century. That, too, classically asserted an over-simple criterion, that of Papal infallibility, which subsequent discussion has qualified extensively by insisting on the co-operation of Bishops and on a *consensus fidelium*, the extent of whose ramifications grow ever more complex.

Unless I am very much mistaken the Church of England is also a church under pressure, and one can certainly hear opinions advanced in favour of radically simplified canons and structures of authority. We have, however, a long history of *not* simplifying these matters. We could do very much worse than ponder the highly differentiated account of authority given by Richard Hooker in the late 16th century. For him divine wisdom is imparted to humanity in diverse ways, not in one, and the interpretation of the Sacred Scriptures requires the divine endowment of reason, in persons consulting, discussing and reasoning together in the community of the faithful.

(iv) *Any* authority without consent is tyranny. This applies as much to a synodical process, as to a direct form of episcopal government. It is of the nature of authority in religious matters, that if it does not acquire recognition, it undermines *de facto* such power as it may have *de iure*. For example, if it were to be in the hands of the bishop of a diocese to fire inefficient parish priests, no matter what his actual powers were, the bishop's decisions would be regarded with disdain if he were thought to be himself intemperate, unreliable and prone to partiality. Members of the General Synod have individually to consider the difficulty there is for a variable elected body, which is necessarily largely anonymous to church members, to establish and maintain a reputation for high spiritual and moral standards. Our Synod exists as an institution in a media context which demands passion, confrontation and spectacular display; every exhibition of folly is guaranteed an instant and dramatic magnification into the homes of hundreds of thousands.

If individual members of Synod behave badly and if Synod as a whole is volatile and unreliable it will simply forfeit that recognition by the Church at large which alone can bestow its moral and religious authority. But exactly the same argument applies to any *de iure* system of government in the Church, whether it be episcopal or congregational. And we may comfort ourselves with the following thought: A church which has survived the Borgia Popes, so our Roman Catholic brothers and sisters tell us, must have received the assistance of the Holy Spirit. A *fortiori*, a church governed by General Synod. Calvin, who was ready to admit that God did indeed use great councils of the church for her guidance, believed nonetheless that even the best of them, such as the Council of Nicaea, were vitiated by exhibitions of human folly. This, he held, was providential. The Holy Spirit, he affirmed, 'so governed the otherwise godly and holy councils as to allow something human to happen to them, lest we should put too much confidence in human beings' (*Institutes* IV, ix, 11).

(v) One final matter needs mentioning, which is the Church of England's attitude towards other Churches, when matters are decided which affect its relationships with them. The consideration of voices from *other* Churches could only be regarded, on the theory which I have been expounding, as part of the normal course of preparation for decision-making. Some Anglicans will think, on good historical grounds, that the separation from Papal jurisdiction imposes a principal obligation to repair that breech ahead of all others. Other Anglicans, on no less good historical grounds, will think that the status of brother – and sisterhood which we enjoy with other parts of the *via media* reformation imposes the major claim. The classic nineteenth-century disputes between rival church parties have imparted to Anglicans a see-saw view of ecumenism, according to which a tilt in one direction implies a tilt away from another. Much of the ecclesiastical politics of ecumenism is conducted precisely on this assumption, and the well-developed bureaucratic party in the Church of England, with large numbers of harassed bishops as paid up members, sees itself in the business of balancing acts, balancing appointments, committees, statements, ecumenical gestures and so forth.

One of the least helpful features of this perhaps inevitable legacy of the theory of "golden mean" is the habit of using relationships with other Churches as a *dis*suasive from pursuing a particular course of action. Of course these relationships matter. They *all* matter, and not just those closest to ourselves. We should make a habit of taking them clearly into account as voices to be heard and opinions to be weighed. But we have no business at all in Christendom if, as Anglicans, we have no confidence in our ability, under the guidance of the Holy Spirit, to think our way through the criteria of authority, to construct a suitable decision-making process, and to commend it to our brothers and sisters in Christ. To say that we have no authority to do X and Y is to make a radically unclear pronouncement; or rather, it is to trade on the sense in which no Christian Church has authority – to alter the Gospel delivered to it – in order to reinforce opposition to proposals which are manifestly (or at least arguably) within its jurisdiction. For to be what the Church of England claims to be, that is to 'belong to the true and apostolic Church of Christ' means to have authority to do what that Church can do. That is why I have argued in this essay not for a theology of authority in the Church of England, but in the Church of Christ. The problems for the Church of England are mostly those common to the whole Church, and we must learn to look not sideways to left and right, but forward to the future, confident that God can call even English Anglicans to set an example of what it means to be faithful and obedient to the vision of his kingdom.

3

The Authority of The Bible

Ruth Etchells

In his Paper *Authority in the Church of England,* Professor Sykes has suggested that the conflict we are currently conscious of in the Church is inherent in the very nature of God's authority, in that while being the sole source of authority, God chooses both that it be 'challengeable' and that it is shared through His gifts with His whole people, who thereby enjoy 'distributed authority', empowered by His Holy Spirit.

In responding to this with particular reference to the authority of the Bible, I want to suggest that the 'tension' or 'conflict' he refers to has more of mystery about it than is suggested by the confrontational language of our times, to which our aggressively polarized culture has habituated us. Indeed, I would go further and say that 'conflict' is the darker and more sinful side of our response to the mystery of the challengeability of God's authority. So I want to use the word 'paradox' to explore the distinctive and empowering nature of God's authority for us. It is actually not the bland word it seems, but a large term with, however, some quite sharp edges. And I find this 'paradox' – that is, opposing truths mysteriously bound together in a larger whole, which our faith is asked to accommodate – when I approach the question of the authority of the Bible.

I want to begin this exploration not with the language of Scripture but with a poem written by Kingsley Amis some 20 years ago. In it he managed to ask most of the questions which lie behind our discussions this weekend, without using, even once, theological jargon. It is based on the game 'O'Grady Says' (which I knew in my youth

26

as 'Simon Says'). You will remember that for this game we all stood in a group and someone appointed used to give commands and if they were prefaced with 'O'Grady (or Simon) says', then we all had to do it, and if they weren't, then we didn't.

Amis calls his poem:

*The voice of Authority: A language game**

Do this. Don't move. O'Grady says do this.
You get a move on, see, do what I say.
Look lively when I say O'Grady says.

Say this, shut up, O'Grady says this
You talk fast without thinking what to say.
What goes is what I say O'Grady says.

Or rather let me put the point like this
O'Grady says what goes is what I say
O'Grady says: that's what O'Grady says.

By substituting you can shorten this
Since any god you like will do to say
The things you like, that's what O'Grady says.

The harm lies not in that, but in that this
progression's first and last terms are I say
O'Grady says, not just O'Grady says.

Yet it's O'Grady must be out of this
Before what we say goes, not what we say
O'Grady says. Or so O'Grady says.

I have chosen this poem because it indicates for us that the issues we are dealing with are inherent in what it is to be human, and that even while being phrased in non-religious ways, they are in the end religious in nature. And because what this poem stresses, as a priority, are that issues concerning authority are relational in nature; it is about a voice or voices engaging with others in a

---

* (Copyright 1956 Kingsley Amis. Reprinted by permission of Jonathan Clowes Ltd., on behalf of Kingsley Amis.)

directive way, and how those others respond and on what grounds. But clustering round that theme are other more searching questions: about intrinsic authority or invited authority, shared authority, and whether humanity should not in the end simply find its own authority in its own present experience and understanding, and nothing more: whether it is not running for cover to commandeer some external non-provable authority as a way of validating the present speaker's judgement and direction.

And this exposes for us some of the questions we face as we examine the authority of the Bible. How far does it have intrinsic authority and how far is its authority attributed to it by an agreed group convention? In what ways does the Church commandeer that authority and in what ways does it sit under it? That is – putting the questions in a more familiar guise: how far does Scripture *describe* the authority of God and how far does it *embody* it? In what ways does its authority reflect the challengeability with which God has proposed Himself to us? How does it stand over against the Church? And how are we to appropriate the authority of Scripture, take it into our corporate and individual lives?

Let us begin with the inherent, intrinsic authority of the Bible. Here is a statement (as it first appeared in the Venice Report of 1976 and was thence fed into the Final Report of ARCIC). Affirming that God has given all authority in heaven and earth to Christ as Lord, the document states that in Jesus the apostolic community came, through the gift of the Holy Spirit, to recognize the saving activity of God, and that they were called to proclaim to all men the good news of salvation. Therefore, they preached Jesus, through whom God has finally spoken to men. And it is here the document bears directly on our question:

> Assisted by the Holy Spirit they transmitted what they had heard and seen of the life and words of

Jesus and their interpretation of His redemptive work. Consequently the inspired documents in which this is related came to be accepted by the Church as the normative record of the authentic foundation of the faith. To these the Church has recourse for the inspiration of its life and mission; to these the Church refers its teaching and practice. Through these written words the authority of God is conveyed. Entrusted with these documents, the Christian community is enabled by the Holy Spirit to live out the gospel and so to be led into all truth. It is therefore given the capacity to assess its faith and life and to speak to the world in the name of Christ.

That is a statement about the authority of Scripture to which our Church has recently given recognition: what is implied in it? Clearly we begin from the intrinsic and final nature of the authority of God Himself; and this authority is vested by God (not, notice, by us), in Jesus Christ our Lord. and it is *this* authority which is 'conveyed' – careful word! – through these written words of Scripture.

And here at once we begin to experience the paradox and nature of God's authority. For His intrinsic authority is present in Scripture in the direct work of the Holy Spirit, not only in inspiring the creation of the documents but in the process of their becoming part of the canon. Yet that creation and that process were *also* achieved by means of communities of believers: by the Jewish community of the faithful which had over centuries created and recognized the Scriptures of the Old Testament; by the apostolic community which transmitted what they had heard and seen of Jesus and their interpretation of His redemptive works; by the community of the Church in the first three or four centuries AD which received, conserved and finally in recognition gave its own authorization in the name of Jesus Christ – in the power, that is, of its distributed authority – to the selection of documents we now hold, collectively, as Holy Scripture.

This is not an 'either/or' process, but one of 'both/and'. There is direct inspiration of the Holy Spirit: there is the collaborative work of the company of believers. And we therefore find, early in our thinking about the authority of Scripture, the paradox. On the one hand there is the absolute and final authority of the inspiration of the Godhead itself: on the other that work is not only known through, but achieved by means of, the fallible and controversial activities and understanding of Christian men and women engaged together under the Lordship of Christ in the work of the Kingdom. And indeed, the existence of Scripture at all is testimony to the paradoxical nature of God's authority, for in it God the unknowable chooses to make Himself known: and in so doing exemplifies the relational nature of His authority.

All this, while being a necessary prelude to our wrestling with some of the current issues concerning the Authority of Scripture, has not really taken us to the heart of our present difficulties, though it supplies, I believe, an approach. For the paradox to which it draws our attention is that, consistently, of the relational aspect of authority.

And here a whole cluster of questions arise. First, and most obvious: if authority is primarily relational, does this mean that if it is not recognized, it ceases to be authority? Does this mean that God does not have authority unless we acknowledge it; and – by analogy and consequence – that Scripture does not have authority unless we accord it?

There is, of course, a profound fallacy here which is at bottom a theological one. For God does not put the reality of His authority at the mercy of our non-recognition: that would evacuate the meaning of the 'God'. Rather He puts Himself at the mercy of our choice not to recognize it. It is God who draws into His Very Being – on the Cross – the cost to Him of non-recognition of His authority. If we consider the Crucifix-ion we find that Jesus humbly endures – as in much of His ministry – the humiliation and rending of spirit which attends the rejection and non-recognition of His authority, *while never for a second withdrawing the absolute-ness of His claim.* The Cross is the ultimate expression of the reality of the authority of God which suffers humbly non-acknowlegement and yet unwaveringly holds by the truth of that authority. And the authority of the Cross is irrefutable.

That is: God's authority is operative in and through non-recognition, effective in and through non-recognition, in salvation history. God's authority remains undiminished, but we ourselves, who can only bloom and bear fruit fully as we appropriate that authority within our own lives, can evacuate for ourselves the power and effectiveness of that authority in what we might have become in the Kingdom. That is the myste-rious paradox of God's faithfulness to the relational nature of authority.

And the authority of the Bible bears the same stamp. Since Scripture is a unique way in which He makes Himself known, it therefore reflects the nature of the God who is making Himself known and the kind of authority He claims. Therefore it retains its authority whether it is acknowledged or not, but it must be acknowledged if it is to be effective in our lives and bear fruit in our growth. It is, like the Lord whose grace it conveys, both accessible to us – that is, to be known and relevant to us – and vulnerable to us – that is, opaque and not generative of power in us – according to our choice.

But even if we do accept the principle of the authority

of the Bible we find ourselves still in the midst of the cluster of questions. Primary among these is a hermeneutic question. That is, what if we accept in principle the authority of the Bible as reflecting in its nature the authority of God, yet by our divergencies of interpretation seem to evacuate that authority of all substance? And again, in what sense can the Bible which God made available *through* the believing community, *stand over against* the believing community in its authority, be normative as a means of judging matters of faith and order? Related to these are all sorts of sub-questions, such as how the Bible in the original intention of its documents may actually be heard today authoritatively through the muffles of distanced intention, transcription, collation and cultural shifts? How may we accommodate the disjunct findings of historical and critical scholarship and the discordant reading, which emerge? How may we sit under the authority both of the individual text and the total canon to which it now belongs, and do these authorities differ? All these questions, and others too, are inevitably implied in any discussion of the authority of the Bible.

Let us remain faithful to the principle which has guided us thus far as a means by which we approach the question, the principle that the *kind* of authority God has shown must be normative in questions concerning authority in Scripture. This provides us with a hermeneutical guide on several issues.

First, just as the Scriptures were created and achieved not simply by means of this or that one man, but by the Holy Spirit working through the interaction of believers, so their interpretation and understanding is a matter for the whole company of the faithful also. It is a 'hermeneutic of the whole Church' to which we are called. And this is the whole Church through time as well as space. We must think not simply of interpretation of Scripture as belonging to our whole parish – as it does; or to that parish as part of the whole Church of England or the whole Anglican Communion – as it does; or to the whole community of God's people at this point in time across the world – as it does; but to the whole of that community through time and forward into the future also. And therefore, *of course*, there will always be different – and opposing – voices since they will reflect the diversity of the whole Church.

But here I want to respond to Stephen Sykes's moving affirmation of the proper sovereignty of every member of the believing community. For such dispersed authority involves every member in precisely the same obligations of suffering rejection as he pointed out were the proper lot of those more usually recognized as wielding authority. In other words, dispersed authority is not *fragmented* authority not the authority of maverick individualism, but rather it is that of responding to each other in counsel, offering and receiving understanding rather than bludgeoning each other with our views.

And this acknowledgement of differing voices within the whole Church leads us at once, and sharply, to the problem of diversities of exegesis which go beyond differing emphases and propose to us opposed and virtually incompatible interpretations. Our 39 Articles charge us that the Church may not 'so expound one place of scripture that it be repugnant to another.' (Article 20). Professor Oliver O'Donovan suggests that the Reformers had 'sufficient experience of diversifying expositions of Scripture to know that they had negative implications for the question of authority. They knew it was not enough to assert the authority of the sacred text and simply leave the hermeneutical question wide open.'* And one must add sadly, they rightly noted the potential for error

* *On the Thirty-Nine Articles*, Oliver O'Donovan, Paternoster, 1986, pp. 56, 57.

within the Church itself. Hence they insisted on the ordinary readability of Scripture, what we call 'Scripture in its plain meaning', and thus implied its potential harmonious reading.

But, as Oliver O'Donovan has pointed out, this is where we cannot go entirely with them, since we ourselves cannot 'impute a sceptical intention to every diversifying interpretation of Scripture'. For, in spite of all the loss that has attended our divergent exegesis, 'the scepticism' bred 'on a large scale', the 'painful loss of confidence in Scriptural authority', the 'petulant wilfulness in theological utterance at every level, from the most scholarly to the most popular', in spite of all these, he insists, we have made a positive discovery: 'that reading for contrast rather than reading for harmony can be wonderfully illuminating of the text'.

For, he argues, the principle which properly lies behind this is that God works His salvation history through our human history, with all its contradictions, oppositions and dislocations. What historical and critical study has shown us of the divergencies and discordant theologies apparent within the whole canon of Scripture is inherent in the very nature of human history which God chooses to use: but the unity of His purpose contains the divergencies. And it is only when belief fails in this unity of God's saving purpose – as fail it has done, in too many readings – that error follows and contradiction rather than faith controls our reading.

This seems to me to offer the beginnings of a way through our unhappy sense of an agreement on the authority of Scripture, and yet a misappropriation of it in divergent readings which seem to rob that claim of substance. It begins from confidence: confidence that Scripture uniquely and reliably testifies to the emerging salvation history of humankind through God's saving acts. It recognises that confronting and divergent theologies are discoverable in Scripture, inevitably so, in that it truly records the perceptions and salvation discoveries of different groups of God's people at different points of their history as they respond to His works; but these are unified by the principle, in the famous formula of Luther, that they are all part of 'what preaches and promotes Christ'. That is the reason for the presence of any document in the canon: that is the nature of its inner unity: that is the basis on which it has come to us.

I would, however, want to go further than this. Our salvation history is indeed reflected in all its human disjunction in Scripture. But unifying it and refusing contradiction within it are authorities which inhere in every just interpretation. They are the authority of event, the authority of person, the authority of word. And each of these authorities within the text of Scripture answers to the kind of authority we have already seen as that of God. That is, the conjunction of the eternal with the temporal; of the divine with the human: of the numinous with the prosaic. God's authority is known and taken up into the shared authority of His people in His name. We must never lose sight, in this mysterious paradox, of both aspects of this: that is, that He is known in and through His people; but that it is not His people only who are known, but *Him*. Interpretation of Scripture can therefore never soundly be reductionist. A right reading of it demands faithfulness both to the marvellous and the mysterious – the inexplicable in human rationalist terms – and to the human community among which the marvellous and mysterious is taking place. Hence an exegetical principle which assumes that event, person or word can reflect only the nature of a human community and not the mystery of divine power at work in it, will be a faulty exegetical principle. We may not, for instance, assume that a fragment or story is inspired within a community solely or even primarily by the need to give some divine dimension to their understanding of their Lord. Since this is the record of God's dealings with His people, the divine is inherent, within the event, the person and the word. We may expect the marvellous and mysterious running with the human and prosaic.

Hence the need to sit before the authority of event, person, word, not only as refracting the changing understanding and perceptions of the emerging Jewish nation or the emerging early Church, but as revealing that which cannot be known, the mystery of God Himself.

How may we do this? How we may appropriate for ourselves in our own times, with sharpness, not the community amongst which the text arises, but the very God of whom it speaks. This is a subject in itself of differences amongst us. Of the opposed voices I want to give simply two extreme examples. One is that of Peter Mullen, Vicar of Tockwith in Northern Yorkshire, as expressed in an article in *The Times* of last September.* The other is that of Peter Baelz, Dean of Durham, as expressed in a sermon also written last September, on the Feast of St. Matthew.

Peter Mullen argued that where we went wrong, and the reason there was a loss of confidence in Scripture, was because we insisted on interpreting Scripture, on discoursing on its meaning, instead of allowing it to speak directly to us. We therefore reduced it to some inadequate overall summary which avoided the oppositions within it – such as St John giving us a triumphant Christ on the Cross who calls out 'It is finished', while St Mark records only the words 'My God; why hast Thou forsaken me?'. Or, alternatively, we insisted on scholarly explanations of the text and its discordances in a way which rendered it spiritless, empty of religious power. There is, Peter Mullen argues, 'a better way'. For:

* 20 September, 1986.

'Meanings are not to be located 'behind' or 'beyond' the text at all. But how often the theologian or preacher talks as if they were. Thousands of sermons on the Good Samaritan say something like . . . 'and so what Jesus *meant* was . . .' to which the reply is: If Jesus had meant that, why didn't He *say* that? Whereas he refused to give an account of the higher ethical doctrine which ought to underlie social practice. He told a story instead . . . And so with the Divine fiction . . . The Passion narratives are comparably more 'meaningful' than any more theory of the atonement. What would it mean for religion if the reverse were true?'

So, he suggests, since we must not leave the words of Scripture on a pedestal of incomprehensibility, we must re-learn an activity which the modern world has long since despised and rejected:

'That is, we should not seek to comprehend religious texts . . . but to appropriate them. That will involve learning them by heart, concentrating on pace and rhythm, devoting ourselves to the task as 'whole men wholly attending'. In this way, the texts become part of us, build us 'by patience and comfort of Thy Holy word'. We do not comprehend them, but they comprehend us . . . when we appropriate our religious texts by heart . . . we find that they truly describe us, search us out and know us. And we know as we are known: reader and text – deep calls into deep . . .'

. . . We are lucky to find that, beyond all the glib 'explanations' the stuff that can really nourish us is still intact. As W.H. Auden once said, 'Why spit on our luck?'.

Now in fact that approach, long lost in the same

cultural context that has also lost the learning by heart of great poetry and great prose, is very closely in alignment with the intention of those 39 Articles I quoted from earlier. The reforms of the 16th century (as Professor Sykes touched on in his Paper) included the placing of a Bible in English in every parish church. And the reformed lectionary emphasized the key place in liturgy of the reading of Scripture, the attending to the actual text rather than a discourse about it. I want to propose that *one* of the ways in which we answer the question 'how may Scripture stand over against, as normative, the community of believers in whose context Scripture was created and authorized' is quite simply by listening to it: by allowing the actual words to address us. For – and I shall come in a moment to an opposing viewpoint – it is these words and not some other which have under the Spirit's dispensation come to us. These words and not some other. Therefore they demand, as Steiner said of every true reading, a condition on the part of the reader of 'tensed delight before the word'.

But of course this alone won't do: . . . it isn't in itself, wholly adequate. For one thing the words we hear are not the words as they would be heard by the hearers in the original situation. So we have to work at recovering the actuality of the original thrust of the words; and that means struggling with analyses of form, with historic accretion with cultural context, and so on. Which brings me to the opposed viewpoint Peter Baelz expressed in his sermon last St Matthew's Day. He reminded us that the Bible was opaque, its meaning not immediately accessible. And he took as an example the text 'For the Son of Man came to call not the righteous but sinners to repentance'.

He pointed out that the Greek verb translated 'to call' had also the meaning of 'to invite'. That the phrase 'to repentance' was not present in some older manuscripts: it could well have been a gloss added to make sure we have got the putative point.

But, we might well ask, what was the putative point? Could it not be that 'the Son of Man came to invite not the righteous but sinners' – for they that are whole need not the physician, but they that are sick.

And therefore, he suggested, apart from the force of this – that we are all invited in that we are all sinners – *the salvation in Scripture is in our wrestling with it so that it speaks to our very hearts*: through the labyrinth of accumulation, critical reading and counter reading, we wrestle with it.

And if we needed it, we have Scriptural justification for such exegesis of its own words; in Acts 8 vv. 36–39, for instance, where Philip asks the eunuch if he understands what he reads and the answer is 'How can I, unless someone guides me?'. And, of course, the great and model exegesis for us is recorded in Luke 24, where on the walk to Emmaus the Resurrected Jesus, 'beginning with Moses and all the prophets, (He) interpreted to them in all the Scriptures the things concerning Himself'.

Now I have quoted those two proposed and opposed ways of appropriating Scripture's authority because they seem to me to be joined in the very paradox of Scriptural authority we have been talking about. The first was emphasizing the mystery of the actual text and its creative power, the fact that the Holy Spirit led us to these words and no other, and that Scripture speaks to us of the mystery and marvel of God in language which is not a 'series of competing propositions' but is instead story, character, meditation, proclamation, drama and poetry. All these embodying the authority of God in Scripture.

The second was reminding us that God used the believing community to produce the men who wrote the Scriptural documents, and He used the believing community, too, in attesting them. The Scriptures owe the context of their authority both to the direct authority of God in acting through the Holy Spirit, and also to the distributed authority of the people of God through whom we have received them. In this paradox neither way of appropriating Scripture authoritatively is misplaced; neither way in itself alone does justice to both aspects of Scriptural authority. We need both.

And so I would suggest a series of paradoxical statements to describe (not define) the authority of Scripture:

– it is *inclusive*, not exclusive: yet *particular*.

(That is, it is about all humankind and it addresses all humankind: yet it is about particular events in particular times and places which are the enactment of God's love relationship with humanity and His saving of His people.)

– it is *dynamic*, not static: yet *constant*.

(That is, there is in every generation more truth and light, as Miles Standish said, to break forth from His word, which has continuing power to move men's hearts in changing cultures; yet its message is constant and not to be changed, and therefore not to be added to or subtracted from.)

- it is *organic*, not external; yet *formal*.

(That is, the authority is inherent in the very nature of Scripture itself, rather than in the externals of differing word orders of translations or languages, yet its formal documentary nature, and the relationships of these documents to each other within the canon, are a part and a real part of that authority.)

– it is *eternal*, not transient and yet *temporal*.

(That is, its authority is drawn from its relationship with the Lord who is beyond time; and it therefore does not disappear with the passing of generations and cultures. Yet by its appropriation by the Church it is effective temporally and answers to our temporal needs).

– it is *powerful* not helpless: yet *challengeable*.

(That is, it is not an authority put at risk by our non-acknowledgement, yet it exposes itself to the effects of that non-acknowledgement.)

I use these pairs of paradoxes simply to suggest an approach to the very nature of the authority of Scripture. In the end, we have to return to the theme of this Conference: the chilling story of Matthew Chapter 21, where Jesus is asked 'by what authority' He acts, and who gave it to Him. He replies with a counter-question. In their refusal to answer it his questioners are exposed and unable to think of authority other than in political terms of power struggle: and so they in turn get no reply: *for none that Jesus could give would have meaning for them.*

So in our search to locate the nature and source of the authority of Scripture. If we come to it with any pre-disposition, any desire to win a point or substantiate our own side of an argument, to use it, in other words, as part of a power struggle, then its authority is fugitive and cannot be appropriated in our lives. But if we come to it as the very address of God, earnestly desiring that His salvation which it conveys should speak to us in our own history, then indeed its words will seize us with authority, the authority which is of Jesus Christ Himself; and with the disciples on the road to Emmaus, we shall find ourselves saying, 'did not our hearts burn within us while He talked to us on the road, while He opened to us the Scriptures?'

4

The Authority of Reason and Conscience

Peter Baelz

To appeal to reason and conscience is not to set up some third source of Christian truth apart from the Scriptures and the Church, but to stress the way in which, under God's good providence, that truth is to be recognized, appropriated and obeyed.

In the conduct of practical affairs decisions have to be made and power exercised. Where more than one person is involved, there has to be some device for determining how to make these decisions and exercise this power, whether this is the will of a single person, a simple or two-thirds majority, or the perceived mind of the meeting – none of which, it should be emphasized, should be equated *tout court* with the guidance of the Holy Spirit.

The existence and acceptance of such a device gives to the exercise of power a practical authority. But such authority is itself 'under authority', namely, the authority of truth, or, in Christian terms, the authority of God. Thus derived practical authority can be challenged in the name of truth and God. It has accordingly to establish its credentials. The question now is whether its claim to authority is a valid and rightful claim. No mere reiteration of the claim will answer the question. There can be no by-passing the processes of thought, appraisal, insight and judgement. The appeal must be to 'reason and conscience'.

It is all too easy to reject this appeal and to resort to some expression of power. Those of us who are parents – especially those who were liberal, intellectual and middle-class parents of the fifties and sixties – can well recall how we used to reason very persistently and persuasively with our offspring in order to convince them that it was wrong, say, to pull the cat's tail. But there came a time when our patience was exhausted by the continuous battery of 'Why?' or 'Why not?', and we brought the argument to a swift and sudden end with the illiberal rejoinder 'Because I say so.' No doubt we were doing the 'reasonable' thing. There are occasions when parents are justified in issuing commands without giving reasons for them. But few of us can have been altogether happy with what we were about, for we had knowingly substituted an appeal to *force majeure* for an appeal to the authority of reason.

'But', it may be said, 'parents are only human, while God is God. If God says, "Because I say so", that is a very different matter from my saying "Because I say so." Indeed, it is also a very different matter from the bishop's saying so, or from my conscience's saying so. When God says so, that's the end of the argument. Did not Job have to admit as much after he had been attempting the impossible of arguing with the Almighty?'

Admittedly, the case is different when we move from human to divine authority. But we may still, without presumption, raise the question *how* God exercises his authority. By an act of pure power? By simply saying the word and it is done? Or in some other way? Are we or are we not right to ground ultimate authority in the exercise of power, simply because that power is omnipotence?

When we speak of the authority of God we must keep in mind the being of God as well as the will of God, his character as well as his action. We must discern the kind of authority which God possesses from the ways in which he makes himself known to us. And if we agree that it is in the person and life of Jesus Christ that we see most clearly spelled out before our eyes the character of God himself, then we must re-think in terms of the character of Christ our all-too-human notions of the power of God. In Christ God shows his 'power' most clearly through 'weakness'. His 'glory' shines from a cross. He does not broadcast his authority by an *ipse dixit*, or parade it in mind-shattering miracles. He *commends* himself and his *love* to us by *dying* for us.

Let me here pick up a word used by Professor Sykes. He spoke of the *challengeability* of God. God exercises his authority in such a way as always to allow himself to be challenged. There is nothing in itself misplaced in our asking for a 'sign' of his authority. But the sign God gives us is not some overwhelming and irrefutable proof, either of word or of deed. It does not have about it the 'glory' of a 'nice knock-down argument'. (Humpty Dumpty knew only too well what he expected of 'glory', but he spoke for unredeemed humanity rather than for the humility of God.) The sign God gives us is the 'glory' of the Cross, a sign of truth and love, a sign which appeals to heart and mind, 'reason' and 'conscience'.

What happens when we re-think the authority of God in terms of the divine love rather than of the divine power, and when we re-interpret power in terms of the 'weakness' of love and its refusal to dominate and compel, threaten and dictate? It does not destroy the idea of authority but it transposes it into a very different key. The authority of love is always challengeable, always open to interpretation and misinterpretation. It needs to be recognized for what it is, and tested for what it can impart. It is essentially relational. This does not imply that its authority has to be given to it by some arbitrary act of will or decree from outside. There is an intrinsic reality and goodness in the divine love, expressed and embodied in the person of Christ, which calls out for an answering recognition of human faith and love. We may speak, if we wish, of the intrinsic *authority* of Christ's life and love. But if that authority is to 'have' authority for human beings, it needs the recognition and response of faith, without which it remains incomplete. God puts himself, his truth and his love, at our disposal, not in the sense that our response gives him a character which he does not already possess, but in the sense that we are invited to judge for ourselves, using all our faculties of heart and mind, who and what he is, and what authority we shall allow him to have over our lives.

Since this is so, we may say that the appeal to the authority of reason and conscience does not derive from any idolatrous claims they may make to be in their own right the ultimate source and arbiter of truth – there is no call to give them honorific capitals, Reason and Conscience. On the contrary, it derives from the being and character of God himself, from the way in which he gives himself to the world he is creating, redeeming and fulfilling. There is a remarkable reserve in the divine self-giving. He gives his creatures time and space to become themselves. He calls upon them to discern for themselves the signs of his kingdom. 'What think you of the Christ?' Whereas the operations of omnipotence could produce only slaves and automata, the gifts of Love, freely given and freely received, empower the selfhood of children. In the paradox of grace God's children are, and remain, totally dependent on him; yet at the same time they are called and enabled to become fully themselves, entering upon the 'glorious liberty' which he wills to give them. In this process of self-communication God's appeal is to his children's discernment and response, to 'reason' and 'conscience'. It is the dynamic of *self-giving love* that lends intelligibility to what otherwise, in the logic of mere power, would be an inescapable contradiction.

The response of faith to the presentation of divine love is certainly not the response of abstract and impersonal argumentation. But neither is it the response of blind trust or arbitrary act of will. Rather, it has within itself the seeds of love, the recognition that here is something, someone, that claims our whole self, that calls forth our whole-hearted assent and affirmation. This initial response of love needs then to be worked out in thought and action.

I hope you will allow me to quote from an article I contributed to the recent number of the Epworth Review (January 1987), not because this gives my words some special authority (!), but because it probably expresses as clearly as I can what I am struggling to communicate to you now: 'It does not seem to me to be too wide of the mark to say that the Christian takes the truth of the Christian gospel on trust. He accepts it on authority. But the authority on which he accepts it is not the authority of infallible knowledge, whether this is ascribed to the Scriptures or to the Church, or even to charismatic experience. Nor is his trust uncritical and unquestioning. Rather it is trust in the recognized authority of love, namely, God's love for his world, embodied in the person of Jesus Christ, reflected in the Beloved and Loving community of the Church, and expressed in the manifold but paradigmatic witness of that community's Scriptures.'

Recognition of the authority of Love does not inhibit reflection, assessment and judgement. It invites them. It may indeed be said that the response of love, if it is to be *truly* loving, requires the ascetical discipline of reason and conscience in order to purify and direct what may otherwise become inverted into sentimentality and illusion. Reason and conscience are rightfully the servants of love, not love's masters nor love's enemies.

The ground of truth, and hence the source of authority, is God himself. But in the humility of his self-giving God accommodates himself to the personal being of his human creatures. His authority, therefore, is essentially relational. It is mediated through human apprehension and appropriation. It becomes challengeable. Expressed negatively, there is no room for infallibility this side of the Parousia. Infallibility is an eschatological concept. Humanly speaking, all authority is fallible. This does not mean that no authority is ever reliable. Nor does it mean that the words of Scripture and the decisions of Church councils lack authority simply because, as human words, however inspired, they too are not in principle exempt from error. Indeed Scripture has a unique authority as primary testimony to God's self-giving in Jesus Christ. And the tradition of the Church has a unique authority as the continuing, critical and constructive reflection on God's self-giving both in Christ and in the life which is in Christ. Nevertheless, when one is asked to give a reason for one's faith and hope, a simple appeal to Scripture and tradition cannot be the whole of one's answer. Some attempt has to be made to answer the question what exactly it is that they say, how it is to be understood, and why it is to be believed. Their authority has to be mediated through heart and mind. It has to be recognized, accepted and appropriated. In theological terms, the truth of God in Jesus Christ is communicated through the inner testimony and conviction of the Holy Spirit.

As will, I trust, have become obvious, I have linked the authority of reason and conscience with the claims of Christian liberty, the 'glorious liberty of the children of God'; and I have linked the claims of Christian liberty with the self-giving love of God. This liberty is not 'the freedom of the subjective person to do as he pleases', but 'the freedom of the responsible person to act as he must' (Michael Polanyi, *Personal Knowledge*, 1958). This latter freedom does not thrive when it contains itself in splendid isolation; on the contrary, it thrives only when it is responsive to the loving invitation and influence of God. The liberal tradition in the Church of England is most truly itself, not when it tries to exist separately from the evangelical truth of the gospel or the catholic tradition of the church, but when it is both critically and constructively responsive to them.

I have now said most of what I want to say about the way in which the appeal to the authority of reason and conscience is grounded in the character and self-giving of God. My concluding remarks will be concerned with the way in which that authority finds expression, especially in the relation between the individual and the community.

It is sometimes assumed that the appeal to conscience is an appeal to something essentially 'private' over against the claims of the community. Although this contains an element of truth, in so far as conscience has its seat in the feelings and judgements of individuals, and is most apparent when an individual cannot 'in conscience' go along with the wishes of the majority, nevertheless to call conscience 'private' – or 'cut-off', which is what 'private' means – is thoroughly misleading. An individual must, if he is to be a person of moral integrity, act according to his own conscientious judgement, whether this prompts him to accept or to reject the views of the majority. But conscience is no infallible inner voice. It is not a Jiminy Cricket. It is not even a private line of communication with God. It is the responsive and responsible judgement of the individual, set in the context of a responsive and responsible community. Certainly, conscience is personal, but it is not 'private'. The individual must make his own judgement, but he cannot arbitrarily determine the criteria on which the judgement is to be based. These criteria are inter-personal and communal. Even the prophet who speaks out against the practices of a community has his roots in the tradition of that community. Were it not so, the prophetic voice of condemnation would carry no appeal and no authority: it would be bare denunciation and abuse.

Nor does Christian belief in the guidance of the Holy Spirit affect the truth of what I have just said. The work of the Holy Spirit is no more 'private' than the judgement of conscience. I well remember the phrase used by C.F.D. Moule, when he was writing about the way in which the Holy Spirit might be expected to work. It was through the 'Christian worshipping congregation listening critically.' And he insisted that each of these five words must be given its full and proper value. Of course, this could be interpreted in such a manner that the individual seems to have disappeared completely within the body of the congregation. But that is not what Professor Moule meant. Rather, the congregation, or community, is made up of individual persons in relation to one another, each listening and responding to the other, and all together listening and responding to God, on the basis of a common worship and a shared faith in the one Lord Jesus Christ.

Practically speaking, however much individuals within a community may reason together and listen to each other's views, disagreement and conflict may still occur. When this happens, conflict has somehow or other to be resolved despite the disagreement. It may be possible to reach a compromise. If a vote is taken, it may be the accepted practice for the minority to give way to the majority. It is always necessary to bear in mind the fact that, however clear and compelling one's convictions, they may be mistaken. But there will still be some issues – those which are often called, too narrowly, 'matters of conscience' – on which an individual cannot give way without going against his deepest self and, as he honestly believes, the prompting of God. When this happens, there may be nothing for it but for the community to be broken – for a schism to occur. But a community which is bound together by allegiance to a common Lord will do all it can to remain, somehow or other, at some level, joined together, even if in certain respects its members have to go their separate ways. Sometimes it can be a sign and expression of love for one's neighbour to keep, at least temporarily, out of one's neighbour's way.

Love and truth, in Christian discipleship, are inextricably bound together. Reason and conscience are the God-given means of discerning that truth and responding to that love. They claim no infallibility. They recognize their own limitations. And if they recognize analogous limitations in the traditions of the Church, and even in the words of the Scriptures, it is because they find their ultimate authority in the living Christ, who is Lord both of Scriptures and of Church. This authority is in the continually renewed 'givingness' of God, rather than in any 'givens' which have been appropriated and expressed in human thought and words. In Alfred North Whitehead's often quoted words: 'Christ gave his life; it is for Christians to discern the doctrine.' Christ still gives his life. Hence the givingness of God is expressed in the whole life of Christ, life in the Spirit. Within this life scripture and tradition will shape Christian identity and give Christian direction; but they should not be expected to determine once and for all every matter of belief and action. It is the Holy Spirit who guides the Beloved and Loving community into all truth. And in this offering and response reason and conscience have their own special part to play.

5

The Authority of The Church, Universal and Local

Adrian Hastings

In regard to the Church the authority of the Church is, in a very real sense, final. Every other authority – reason, the Bible, God – has to be mediated within it, through it, so that if the Church is the most rightly judgeable of all things (from that to which most is given, most will be expected), so is the Church too the judge of all things. To it has been given the keys of the kingdom, the power to bind and to loose. In the context of the Church this must needs be so, though not in the context of the individual and in regard to the individual. Here the private conscience is equally final, and all other authorities must needs be mediated through that, even the voice of God. But there is no way in which the Church as a recognizable and public body, a fellowship of women and men joined by sacrament, belief and common purpose, can evade the requirements of its own authority. However much it may proclaim and be conscious of its subordination to God and to revelation, it is still, within its on-going life, the Church itself which decides the relationship of revelation to Bible, the frontiers between Bible, reason and experience, how God has spoken and how God's word has this here and now implication and not another. It may appeal to the power of the Spirit, it may pray, it may cast lots, it may discuss, it may vote, it may consult the faithful or limit its debates to the bishops, it may leave all to the Pope or nothing to the Pope, but in none of these ways can it avoid the simple truth and basic responsibility of its own authority without thereby ceasing to be the Church.

51

All this is the more obvious when we are concerned with such issues as those of ministry, the who and how of ordination, the authority of synods. These are, most eminently, Church matters: they have no standing at all, no sense apart from the Church and precisely because they are essentially – and in no derogatory way – so churchy, the authority which the Church possesses must be exercisable in regard to them most appropriately.

Nevertheless this is not, of course, the primary area of concern for Church authority. Far from it. The Church is a missionary, preaching, witnessing body. What power it has it must exercise, first of all, in witnessing to the Father of Our Lord Jesus Christ, the death and risen life of Jesus, the power of the Spirit, the meaning of reconciliation, the life of justice and holiness to which in Christ mankind is called. All this comes first by sheer ecclesial necessity. It did and it does. But the exercise of that witnessing, the internal guidance of the communion of the faithful, the structure and handing-on of the ministry across the generations, into new lands and an ever-widening circle of the faithful – numerical, geographical, linguistic – required a secondary exercise of Church authority, in matters then which were not so much given to the Church as generated within the Church's history, matters over which the Church should appropriately exercise a conscious control which it does not have in the primary area. It is not accidental that in the course of Christian history and theology, the doctrine and theology of the sacraments, of the ministry, of the very nature of the Church and its authority are rehearsed, take some sort of formal shape and are (occasionally) even 'declared' far later and far more accidentally, pragmatically and indecisively than the doctrine and theology of God, Christ, redemption, grace. They are tools rather than ends; servants not saviours; socially and culturally conditioned and reconditioned in a way that – it is true –

our grandparents seldom appreciated but which we, fortified by the historical and anthropological perspectives of the modern mind, cannot ignore. The conditioning is not an invention of our time, only in some sort a discovery.

The Church, then, is and always has been struggling to update, to shape and reshape its consciousness and structured ministry so to be able here and now to fulfil, with as little unworthiness and ineptitude as may be (yet it will still be with much, being composed of unworthy servants) its single calling in new, changing and varied circumstances. The struggle to do all this is not new. It has been there since, precisely, apostolic times. And because of the intrinsic nature of this whole area of Church life and ministry, the pragmatic development of actually living and ministering has somehow to predate the authorization of the Church, especially of the worldwide Church. So it always was. The Church did not begin with a doctrine of ministry. It began with a very simple praxis of ministry which grew and grew and as it grew its branches had to be blessed and pruned – perhaps very occasionally one needed actually to be lopped off. But it was and is of the very nature of Catholic ecclesiology and ministry that the development preceded the formal and ecumenical authorization. Even the canon of the New Testament, so decisive subsequently for the life, teaching and self-understanding of the Church came in its authoritative and ecumenical form – and could only come – long after the development within local churches whereby separately written books were linked together and set apart to share a kind of divine and inspired authority already recognized in the books of the Old Testament.

A muddled process in a muddled Church. So it was and so it still will be, if we are going to adhere to a model of a living rather than mummified catholicity, the model of a pilgrim church, whose rules are never quite laid down in advance. Nobody seriously studying the history of Christianity from the second to the fifth century could, I think, doubt the basic truth of that model. Different local churches in communion with one another but with no agreed procedures for settling problems in advance or universally had to feel their way forward when faced with issues which, in the circumstances of the day, required a solution with an urgency which the same issue had not previously seemed to have. In due course the Emperor Constantine pressed upon the Church the practice of an ecumenical council – a boon, if also a curse in the scale of secular political influence it witnessed to. But it came after two hundred and fifty years of coping otherwise – through local councils or the pastoral decision-making of individual bishops, the seemingly haphazard moving forward of the Christian consciousness. And Nicaea did not end all that. The ecumenical council has remained a way of responding to already well advanced developments and disputes rather than a way of plotting out a theoretical line of advance in hitherto unexplored territory and the role of the Papacy at its most beneficial has been mostly of the same sort – what the Second Vatican Council in its Decree on Eastern Catholic Churches spoke of as that of 'supreme judge of inter-church relations' (art 4).

I am assuming, of course, in speaking to you in this way that you, the Church of England (or the Anglican Communion) are genuinely a part of the *Ecclesia Catholica* about which I am talking. Obviously, there would be little point in my being here if I did not do so. But I cannot speak trying to be an Anglican theologian when I am not – trying to think what an Anglican theologian could most reasonably say on this theme and in this predicament, if he or she also happened perhaps to share some of the ideas I myself have. No, that would not do. I can only speak as myself, a Catholic theologian baptized and ordained within the Roman communion and – I trust – still within that communion, even if my own disagreements with its canonical insistances have placed me in an anomalous position within it. Now Pope Paul called you 'a sister Church' and while that was not an infallible statement, it is at least consistent with many others and may be said to represent the praxis of Rome today, even if there is in Rome itself hardly a coherent theology to make full sense of it. Vatican II went some way towards providing one, but not a full way. Since then documents like the Malta Statement and those of ARCIC all stand, upon the Roman side, with at best ambiguous authority. We are out of one ecclesiology but hardly into another. Here again praxis goes ahead of theory. The Church is a communion of faith, sacrament, fellowship, but this communion – Vatican II does tell us – can be partial as well as complete. I take it that in point of fact the true fullness of communion is here and now unrealizable for anyone. There are degrees of holiness, catholicity, unity, also degrees of communion. The partiality of possession of all its other marks is precisely the mark of the Church as historic, a Church on the way to being itself. Of course, not all diminutions of fullness are equally grave. Of course, the Church of England in particular – as this is what we are concerned with now – is, we must certainly recognize, not all that it should be. Of course, it was a grave lack of appropriate communion that at the second Vatican Council there were no Anglican voting members (nor Greek Orthodox either). But that indicates a lack upon both sides and, of course, if it is not hard to point out other Anglican defects, one can hardly deny some Roman ones as well. The point is that, in all sorts of different ways, the Church here and anywhere is *semper reformanda*. Every local church fails to be fully and recognizably what a local church ought to be and yet – so long as its members cling on to Christian faith and baptism, eucharist and creed and penitence for sin, and an unfailing hope in God who is God – it is not and cannot be basically unchurched. A sister Church, in partial communion, is still a local Church. The key fact about the pilgrim Church is that it is not kingdom, it is not perfect, it is not arrived, it is in history, it is in a very real way creating itself as it moves along in the darkness of faith, a company of sinners striving, pretty pathetically most of the time, to be saints as well. The truest ecclesiology will be one very largely of imperfection, fallibility, partial communion.

That, I believe, represents a fair rough picture of Catholic ecclesiology, refertilized by the better insights of Vatican II. And the Church of England may see itself in such a context. In this great *Ecclesia Catholica* it has to recognize and carry its responsibilities as just part of the whole, a local church, an *ecclesia particularis* in the Council's frequently used phrase. You are a local church suffering for historical reasons certain disabilities – (such as non-representation among the voting members of Vatican II) – but also enjoying, even thereby, certain considerable advantages. Above all, you should have now a great freedom, relatively unbound by the restrictions of Roman canon law and control upon the one hand, royal and parliamentary bondage upon the other. Your exceptional freedom could make of you not so much a bridge church, more a pilot church. But basically you might do well to behave – theologically but not canonically – as if you had been at Vatican II. You are a local church. Do not pretend to be the universal Church. The universal Church exists as a communion of local churches and the local church is subject to the universal Church. Hierarchically and sacramentally the wider communion remains a bit upset at present – though not so much as it used to be – but you can only behave responsibly as if it were there. Clearly your Synod cannot claim the degree of authority that a universal council can claim: *Securus judicat orbis terrarum*. Don't forget that (I am not suggesting that you do, I am just reminding you). But, of course, even Vatican II with its 2,000 plus bishops was not fully *orbis terrarum*. It did matter that Constantinople and Canterbury were not there. Alas: We cannot in present circumstances engineer *Orbis terrarum*. If we denied that Constantinople and Canterbury and Moscow had anything to do with the Church except as a matter of history or individual faith and good will we could declare – as we did on the old Roman ecclesiology – that Vatican II and such like were totally ecumenical. Full stop. But we can't. The very words and deeds of the popes, as much as the sheer witness of religious and Christian reality, make that today too difficult. Once we are forced to recognize that the great eastern schism really could not have excluded either Latins or Greeks from the visible apostolic Church, we have to cope with the provisionality of not having a contemporary *orbis terrarum* effectively to appeal to. Yet it remains in principle and in practice more in Vatican II than in Lambeth, yet not wholly in one when it does not include the other.

The Church is a communion of churches and sub-churches – from the house church to the province which links together a group of dioceses. All have their proper ministry and authority. All must see themselves, respectfully, humbly, but creatively and adventurously too, within the wider apostolic *communio ecclesiarum*: to be heirs of the apostles does not simply nor primarily mean to be a repository of apostolic teachings, harking cautiously back to a *depositio fidei*, but to have the sort of adventurous apostolicity which took Peter and Paul out from the established confines of the Church of the circumcision to the challenges and new rule makings of the Church of the Gentiles. Remember that the Council of Jerusalem – our scriptural paradigm for ecclesiastical problem solving – came together and provided a ruling after, not before, the crucial initiatives had been taken locally elsewhere. There were plenty of uncircumcized Christian believers, some among whom had already even been appointed as elders with prayer and fasting (Acts 14.23) before the Council ruled 'It has seemed good to the Holy Spirit and to us to lay upon you no greater burden' (Acts 15.28). Apostolicity really lies in adhering imaginatively to that total model: the courage to take local initiatives, which are sure to be roundly condemned by others as untraditional and unapostolic, as well as the ability to accept in due course the decision of the whole Church when it has been properly reached.

Of course, a local church could not absolutely know that it was not mistaken when it decided that the uncircumcized might be baptized and made elders, or that after persecution *traditores* might be reconciled, or that – despite Paul's teaching in I Timothy – an unmarried childless celibate might be chosen as bishop, or that infants might be baptized, or confirmation separated by years from baptism, or whatever: all more or less revolutionary decisions taken first in fear and trembling by one or another local church, somewhere, sometime, long before the universal Church had 'declared' that it was right.

The local church is not infallible. It may be wrong. It may even be in danger of becoming schismatic if it presses ahead with some missionary or pastoral innovation while the wider Church too strongly disapproves. But, equally, if it does nothing, if it procrastinates indefinitely, when the need is there, it may still more surely come under judgement and dry up like the fig tree, correct but nevertheless fruitless. The point is that new pastoral decisions have got to be taken again and again in the course of history and they cannot initially be taken from the centre or by a general council. Without such decisions the Church is bound to dry up, tied to an anachronistic shape. The guidance of the Spirit is to be seen more in the courage to move than in the prudence which resists innovation. Again and again in history circumstances somehow re-enact that first moving out process from Jew to Gentile. Adhering unchangeably to a previous pattern of ministry until the universal Church decides otherwise is not to follow the apostolic model and is a recipe for ensuring that the universal Church never decides anything. Apostolic fidelity requires, on the contrary, the courage of local churches to jump the gun while doing so utterly unschismatically, determined to maintain all that they can of catholic unity (but not uniformity), aware that there are bound to be painful confrontations – just as there were at Antioch – but clear above all that mission and pastoral need come first and cannot be resolved simply in terms of fidelity to past practice – even in apparently major matters. Catholicism is a living, developing organism of understanding and ecclesial structure or it is nothing. Any sort of fundamentalism which could settle the shape of the Church or the formulas of her faith once and for all in terms of how things were in the 5th century or the 2nd or at the death of the last apostle or whenever, has absolutely to be rejected, and precisely out of fidelity to the growing historical catholicity which has always characterized Christian history, the intrinsic developmentalism of the New Testament itself which presents itself not as closed law but as a model to take with us into the unknown future.

When one considers the relationship of local church authority to universal Church authority, it is impossible to say that some matters can be put into the first box only, some into the second. Many of the greatest doctrinal issues were considered in local councils; quite little pastoral matters could be legislated about in ecumenical councils. Of course, not all that is done is done wisely or rightly. But what we cannot do is to exclude certain types of decision and initiative because, for instance, they are too important to be taken locally. On the contrary, the most important decisions must come locally first. What is required in the councils of the local church is to approach such matters with a sense of high doctrinal and pastoral responsibility – not only for oneself, but for the whole *Catholica*.

Are there no limits we can theoretically pose to the power of the Church, universal or local, to reshape its own constitution and ministry? It is hard to think of many with assurance. There has, undoubtedly, been a strong tendency to want to push back almost all the contents of this secondary category of concern into the primary category, to fundamentalize it, one might say, and of course we can't divide the two completely – the Eucharist and Baptism in particular are essentially bridging elements coming from the one into the other. So too may be a differentiated ministry, as well as a still more especial 'Petrine' thread of authority, or – again – the mediatory power to express the forgiveness of sin even apart from baptism. We have to be careful how we tamper with such as these. And yet, of course, the whole central history of the sacraments and the ministry has been that of one long tampering with such central inheritances. The shape of the Mass, developing over the centuries, and differently with different liturgies, is proof that we can and even have to tamper with them. We could only begin to justify some of the main lines of the medieval Papacy or, again, religious orders with an immensely flexible and developmental kind of ministerial theology. And if we should say – as Roman theology has often tended to say – that some rather precise things we cannot touch: that we cannot, for instance, in any way touch the matter of the eucharist, it has for validity to be wheaten bread, then we would be forced to conclude that the St Thomas Christians in south India, celebrating their eucharist for many hundreds of years wheatless, but using some sort of rice cake instead never really celebrated Mass, renewing the sacrament of the Lord's Supper. They were geographically incapable of so doing. How absurd. How could we think God so foolish! In the later Middle Ages, a number of Popes undoubtedly gave permission for various abbots, who were not bishops, to ordain priests – thus anticipating John Wesley. Again the Council of Florence quite formally declared the 'matter' of the sacrament of ordination to be the 'handing over of the instruments' ('traditio instrumentorum'), a practice which never existed at all before the Middle Ages. All such cases argue emphatically against any sort of sacramental fundamentalism.

A brief consideration of two other issues may help us further in understanding the way the Church has developed, its authority has been exercised and recurring doubts about sacramental validity overcome.

The first is that of confession and absolution. The Church's continual sense of being a community in which sin is forgiven by the power of God has taken a variety of sacramental forms – some more public, some more confidential. The Church at any particular time may prescribe the forms but it is not bound by the forms of other ages. Certainly in the Middle Ages people often confessed their sins to the laity; the last Catholic bishop of Iceland indeed did so to his wife when on his way in 1550 to lay down his life for the faith at the hands of Danish Protestants. That event does not seem outside the frontiers of acceptable Catholic tradition.

The other issue is that of baptism by women, much controverted in the Church of England in the 16th and 17th century. The bishops were anxious to defend the validity of baptism by midwives; some more extreme

Protestants denied that it could be done. It may be that the underlying attitudes and arguments used then and now are not so very different. The traditional Christian insistence that women can baptise coupled with the reluctance of some Christians to allow it to happen has a good deal to say to the question whether, when pastorally opportune, a woman can be ordained.

The moral I would draw from these and other examples is that the Church has the power to construct and reconstruct its ministry, its sacramental forms and hierarchy, and has in fact done so (more or less wisely and imaginatively) according to the culture and pastoral needs of the age – even though it has not for the most part been self-consciously aware of that power. Hugh of St Victor thought there were thirty sacraments. I am not entirely sure that we were wise to agree instead with King Henry VIII (and, of course, many better theologians before him) and declare that there are only seven, and I am not entirely sure that in the future the Church will not profitably reconstruct some of those other twenty-three.

It may be helpful, finally, to point to the way in which the World Council of Churches and its Central Secretariat has developed since the 1940s. Theology did not come first here, at least consciously. What came first was a spiritual aspiration and the response to an international pastoral need, which had at first almost ostentatiously to disavow eccelesiological significance. And yet of course that significance has been enormous in re-establishing, outside the world of the Roman Communion, the sense of the *Ecclesia* as requiring the embodiment of a universal ministry and centre of unity. One might indeed say, paradoxically, that behind modern Geneva is none other than a petrine theology of a 'see of unity': unable to tolerate its present realisation in Rome because of the latter's exaggerated pretensions and practical intolerance it has been necessary to realise it *pro tem* elsewhere. A very ancient theology may then be implicit in this modern praxis, yet almost unconsciously. And that is what one finds again and again. When some seemingly revolutionary development has taken place, one can recognise within it in altered dress the imperious require-ments of the 'faith once delivered to the saints'. So too in some apparently traditional adherence to the precise pattern of the past one may at times only too clearly detect a form of faith crucially at variance with the central message of the gospel.

If a local church – laity, bishops, priests – faced with a need for a radical pastoral initiative, think and reason about it, pray, seek the guidance of God's spirit and then act in such a way as to adapt the structure of the Church and its ministry to express better in today's world Christ's abiding truth, then ecclesiologically it cannot be faulted. Ecclesiologically, it is not wrong because it has not been done before. Ecclesiologically, it is not wrong because the *orbis terrarum* has not yet pronounced upon it. Ecclesiologically it would be wrong, after such a process, to be afraid to act for no other reason than that the universal Church remains partly uncertain, partly opposed. The rightness of the particular decision must be hammered out pastorally, christologically, soteriologi-cally, anthropologically, but not ecclesiologically. Eccle-siologically, the world Church in its full authority can only say to the innovators who have thought it out in those other dimensions, and prayed and gone ahead, 'Brethren, since we have heard that some persons from us have troubled you with words, unsettling your minds, although we gave them no instructions, it has seemed good to us in assembly to send to you with Barnabas and Paul, Judas and Silas . . .' to confirm not just the legality but the immense pastoral and missionary desirability of some seemingly controversial novelty. That, I believe, is what the *Catholica* will in due course say yet again but, of course, 'some persons from among us' may well say quite a lot of other things first.

6

An Agenda For The Church?

Robert Jeffery

One member of the Conference, the Revd David Mowbray of Hertford, responded to Professor Sykes' Paper by
writing a hymn, which was subsequently sung in the
Worship:

Said Jesus to the Twelve,
Be careful how you seek
The power which Princes of this world
Exert upon the weak.

Said Jesus to the Twelve,
No so my Friends with you;
Take up the Task the Son of Man
Has come on earth to do.

Said Jesus to the Twelve,
As servant I am here
To suffer for the world God loves,
To bring his rescue near.

Now let the Church reply,
Amen, so let it be.
Let Christian lives display the mark
Of Christ's Authority.

(Tune: Doncaster)

It caught the mood well. The saying of our Lord: 'But it
shall not be so among you' (Luke 22.26) rang through
the Conference. The Authority of the Church is not the
authority of the world. It is like the authority of its Lord,
vulnerable and open to challenge. When it ceases to be

so, it ceases to reflect the authority of Christ. John Austin Baker expressed this well when he wrote in *The Foolishness of God*:

> Jesus' authority rests on the unique fact of himself. The Church in turn fulfils her calling only as she lives by his spirit, which is God's own spirit; and in so far as she does so, she confronts men with the same challenge . . . The spirit of love has to be accepted on its own merits or not at all; hence the Christian community has authority only by virtue of what it is. (p. 353)

Inevitably the spirit of the Age rubs off upon the Church but the Spirit of God must prevail if the Church is to be the Church. Here was a key provided by the Speakers which led us away from our own entrenched positions into something much more risky. The mood of our Age, epitomized in the late 1960s by Charles Davies, as 'the lust for certitude', just will not do. Openness and vulnerability are signs of the Kingdom. However, this is to move into an area of great anxiety and much of the Conference was spent in working out what this might mean personally and corporately.

Thus in the dialogue with those of differing views we were reminded not simply that we were asking them to be open to challenge but that we needed to realize that 'we are part of the problem'. It was Peter Baelz who reminded us that 'the organ of the Holy Spirit is the Christian worshipping congregation listening critically'. That critical listening must include ourselves. Just as we are all under judgement and all accepted in God's love so we are all vulnerable. We should not be afraid to admit it. So we may be able to face real and deep divisions. One group faced a stark division over the interpretation of Scripture which led to people accusing each other of idolatry. It may be that this was an example of a refusal to accept a 'dispersed authority'. For it is of the very nature of such authority that it cannot be idolatrous just because it is dispersed. The various strands of authority need each other for their fullness. Thus, the closing Act of Worship included more than one dramatic representation of the need to hold Scripture, the Church, reason and experience in a spirit of mutual sharing, not of rejection. This is not a removal of authority from Scripture. It is the acceptance of other authorities and a willingness to allow all authority to be open to examination and question.

Possibly more could have been made of this. The great genius of the Bible is that it can be read in different ways and at different levels. We have no right to expect that all people will read it in the same way. Biblical critics may have been at fault in insisting that there can only be one true interpretation based upon the findings of critical scholarship. The scholars themselves do not agree. A Biblical passage may speak directly to the life of prayer of someone who has no knowledge of the critical approach. There can be a form of academic gnosticism in relation to Scripture. We need to learn from each other and not to claim that any one way of looking at Scripture is the only one. There lies the risk of faith. Thus one group called for honesty of thought and a willingness to criticize the critics. When considering moral issues there is much difficulty in applying the Bible direct; rather we have to take into account the nature of the world, the human situation and the possibilities opened up by redemption. No narrow interpretation will do, and so the group concluded: 'We thought that the deficiencies in the Bible had to be noticed as much as its affirmatives.'

This is not the only area of risk. Members of the Conference were both thrilled and disturbed by Adrian Hastings' strong justification for the view that doctrine follows practice and not the other way round. Does not such an approach lead to disorder? The answer must be that it can and sometimes has got very near to total breakdown. Yet it is the way change takes place. The illegalities of the Ritualistic Movement in 19th-century Anglicanism caused much controversy and bitterness, but they have contributed considerably to liturgical renewal. Similarly, this was the way 'areas of ecumenical experiment' developed during the 1960s. Much in the growing together of local congregations, in shared buildings, worship and ministry has been technically illegal. It has been done, in the main, responsibly.

The amount of resources put into Ecumenical Projects by the Church of England has been very considerable. This has been done in spite of the failure of the Church to implement any Union Scheme. The ecumenical approach has been a response in Mission to a changing situation. In some places it is bearing much fruit. Many of the illegalities are now to be regularized in the new Ecumenical Canons of the Church of England. The Law is catching up after nearly 25 years of practice. It is a good illustration of what Adrian Hastings was pointing to. The President of the Selly Oak Colleges, Martin Conway, commented that this progress had been made through the use of the 'Sponsoring Body' which provided both a 'buffer' and a 'bridge' for the Denominational Authorities. It was a buffer that released denominational resources into an Ecumenical Project; it was a bridge which feeds back the experience into the Denominations. What began as a pioneering idea at the Nottingham Faith and Order Conference of 1964 has now become normative for many.

The matter of the Ordination of Women to the Priesthood was never far from the surface of the Conference. Those in favour will find Adrian Hastings' thesis very attractive. It could well be that the theological implications of the Ordination of Women cannot be fully grasped until women have been ordained. Canon

Christopher Hall reminded us of the actions of his father, Bishop R.O. Hall of Hong Kong, in ordaining the first woman priest in the Anglican Communion in 1944. The events are fully described in Canon David Paton's Biography of R.O. Hall. The action was an expression of what he calls 'The Cornelius Factor'. Like St Peter admitting a Gentile into the Christian Community, Bishop Hall, after much prayer and reflection, felt he could do no other. Whatever has happened since, that action cannot be undone. The first woman priest, Lee Tim-Oi, is now over 80 but still alive to tell her story. That is the way change takes place. From Cornelius onwards that has been the way God has been seen to act. But how do we know that? We do not know it. It is again one of the risks of a vulnerable faith.

Many felt that while there was justification for this approach, the pressures of the Media and the effect of instant news was a bad handicap in enabling change to take place naturally and at a gentle pace. News spreads too fast. People do not need the limelight if they are to change and grow and develop. This is not the whole truth, for from the Acts of the Apostles onwards, it has been by the telling of the stories of what people have done that others have gained the faith and the confidence to go the same way. The story of Jesus is a liberating and encouraging story, which gives us hope and sets us on our way. Certainly, as Henry Chadwick reminds the 1968 Lambeth Conference, there is nothing in the New Testament to make us think that it is wrong to do something for the first time.

But at what level should the Church so act? When is local really local? What is the relation of the Local to the Universal Church? This is a very difficult question. In an Episcopal Church it is the Bishop who represents the universal to the local and vice versa. Adrian Hastings took the view that the local Church might well be the

Church of England, not just a village church in a remote part of England. If this is so then all the checks and balances are already present to prevent some sudden and rash moves in a new direction. Peter Baelz reminded us that Quakers come to a decision not by a vote but by waiting for a common mind to emerge. Whatever the decision the risk is still there – we may make the wrong decision. Not everything that a corporate body decides is right. Here again is the 'risk of faith'. We can here be reminded of 'the Gamaliel principle' (Acts 5.39). If it is a wrong decision we shall soon see. If it is of God it will bear his fruit. There is here a sense of liberation. Anxiety breeds fear; taking risks leads to freedom.

To make good decisions, we need to make them in a wide context. Our thinking is too insular, too turned in on ourselves. It is one of the paradoxes of living in a Global Village, first pointed out by Teilhard de Chardin, that the more the world seems to be one, the more we turn in on ourselves. 'But it shall not be so among you.' Our faith is that the whole world belongs to God and that we share in fellowship in the one Body throughout the world. Both Christopher Hall and Martin Conway reminded us of the remarkable story of the Church in China. We can learn much about our own situation from listening to Chinese Christians. John Allen, the Provost of Wakefield, gave us two images. One was of Archbishop Janani Luwum talking to students not long before his Martyrdom and saying that the Church in Uganda had become too comfortable and needed 'the discipline of persecution'. His other image was that too much church life seemed to be like a circle looking in on itself, instead of outwards to God's world. I could not help reflecting at that point on the circular nature of the Debating Chamber of the General Synod. Perhaps it does turn us in on ourselves. This may be an added reason for the General Synod to move away from Church House!

There are Christians today in many parts of the world who can tell us of 'the discipline of persecution' and we thought and prayed for many of them during the weekend. We had those with us who could tell us of what Christians are undergoing in South Africa, in Nicaragua and in many other places. It is only a Church which is willing, like its Lord, to be challenged and vulnerable, which will be open to the possibility of persecution. Is this why the Church of England has experienced so little of it? It has not been open enough.

The image of the closed circle is the same. How can anyone get in? We heard of several people alienated from the Church because it is so turned in on itself. It has become so self-concerned and so embroiled in its own wrangles that people have looked elsewhere for the Christ. Only a Church which is weak and vulnerable can reveal the attractiveness of its Crucified Lord.

So too we were reminded not to be anxious about conflict in the Church. There never was a time without conflict. As the Church reflects something of the Age in which it is placed, people within it perceive the doctrines, the worship and the Lord himself in different ways. God has made us all different and we need each other's perspectives if we are to move nearer the truth. We should not expect total agreement. Total agreement would be a denial of the weakness and vulnerability of God as we see him in Jesus Christ. As John Austin Baker has put it in the passage previously referred to:

> For there are three things which lie at the heart of Christianity: belief, love and worship – not one of them can be achieved in obedience to authority. They are all free personal commitments or nothing. (*The Foolishness of God*, p. 354)

If our faith is that broad, what keeps us together? For many generations Anglicans rejoiced in the so-called

Lambeth Quadrilateral. (Scripture, the Creeds, the Apostolic Ministry, the Sacraments.) These were backed up by a common allegiance to the See of Canterbury, an acceptance of the Thirty-Nine Articles of Religion and the Book of Common Prayer. We see this much less clearly today. The Ordination of Women to the Priesthood has ruptured the sense of full Communion with Canterbury, the revisions of the Declarations of Assent have reduced the significance of the Thirty-Nine Articles; Church Union Schemes and the general pattern of Ecumenism has undermined assurance in a given pattern of Episcopal Ministry. Liturgical Revision has moved the uniform acceptance of the Book of Common Prayer. Moreover, Professor Sykes in his Paper pointed to the radical shift which has been taking place throughout Christendom as a result of the Second Vatican Council. What then does hold us together?

Adrian Hastings' answer is that it lies not in a common agreement but in a common sharing in the Sacramental Fellowship of Baptism and Eucharist. He is making a powerful point. The New Testament Christians did not always agree but they broke bread together. The growing ecumenical convergence on the meaning of Baptism and Eucharist as revealed in the World Council of Churches Lima Document (*Baptism Eucharist and Ministry*) give this emphasis real substance. Moreover, it is also reflected in the ARCIC documents and in other bilateral Union Conversations around the world. We are held together by the objectivity of Sacramental Union rather than by the subjectivity of the acceptance of professions of faith or rigid doctrinal formulae. This point was drawn out by Rubem Alves in his book *Protestantism and Repression* (SCM Press 1985). He points out that the difference between a Catholic and a Protestant view of the Church lies just here. Protestantism sees a basis in a common Confession of Faith, which inevitably means excluding people. Catholicism expresses its basis in a Sacramental Union, which can embrace people with very different views. Thus, many Roman Catholics have profound differences but they remain united through the Sacrament. Here again we see the vulnerability of Christ. It is in the Sacrament that we share in Christ's death and resurrection. It is in the Sacrament that we come face to face with the vulnerability of God. This was well-expressed by that great Anglo-Catholic protagonist Bishop Frank Weston:

> So many people go to Communion seeking peace. We go into His presence, whose hands are marked with nails and we ask for peace. And we get no peace, because we ought rather to ask for that deeper sense of His presence as He leads us into war. Reach out your hands to receive His Body and your hands will be marked with the wound. And each communion as you make it faithfully, you will find our Lord preparing for you some new wound. There is always something more in our nature which he wills to mark with the Cross.

That is true of the Church as well as of the individual Christian. Communion with Jesus Christ makes us more vulnerable, more open to challenge, more willing to admit we may be mistaken, more willing to suffer for his sake. So our divergence of views, our contradictions, our confrontations all unite us in the vulnerability of God Himself.

Those who attended the Conference from other groups in the Church of England attested to this during the final Eucharist. The hope was expressed that future Conferences might be organized jointly. As we get to know each other, the caricatures of each other fade away. This does not mean that we end up agreeing with each other but it does enable us to enter into Communion together.

Thus, the Conference ended with an extended Eucharist in which all had the opportunity to contribute their insights. We sang and prayed with fervour and with meaning. Canon Ivor Smith Cameron, using gifts acquired over many years of work with small groups, led our worship with sensitivity, with a subtle mixture of silence, incense, recorded music, choruses and sharing, he helped us all to come together in worship of our one Lord. It was an Act of Reconciliation, through which ran the same theme: 'But it shall not be so among you'. The authority of Christ is an open, deep, vulnerable, loving authority to which we can respond with freedom.

What then have we learned? What is the Agenda? I had come to the Conference faced with the words of a wise, retired ecclesiastic, who posed the question: 'What does the centre stand for? Where is it going?' Does is stand for change for change's sake rather than taking a stand on the roots of Faith, as one observer claimed? This is not the way I would see it. What we were doing was seeking to go back to the roots and seek Christ's authority and not our own.

But many do not wish to go that way. They find an attraction in firm views and strong dogmatic assertions. They like to know where they are. That is what the Media have been looking for from the Church, but it must be resisted. It is the security sought by adolescents. In his *God of Surprises* Fr Gerard Hughes has taken us back to Baron von Hugel and his insistence that we need to hold in balance the institutional, the critical and the mystical elements of religion. We cannot do without any of them and we cannot emphasize one element at the cost of the others. The adolescent looks for the security of the institution but shies away from the threat of the critical.

Nor can we dare to neglect the mystical growth in spiritual maturity which will take us into many a 'Dark Night'. Such a balanced view does not attract those with a 'lust for certitude'. But neither does a balanced view repel in the way that the over-dogmatic can repel. The centre needs to be a lot less apologetic for being central. It seeks to hold in tension things with otherwise fall apart. What then typifies this central position? From the Conference we may note the following aspects:

An acceptance of conflict as creative

A realism about the way we are caught up in our own Age

Understanding the need for risk

Turning to the wider world and being willing to listen

An acceptance of a dispersed authority where all is open to challenge and all must be held together

A willingness to enter into dialogue with those of differing views

A desire to communicate the Gospel with intellectual integrity

An awareness that we may be wrong or mistaken – and so may everyone else

A pattern of prayer and worship which leads us closer to God in Christ Jesus and accepts his standards, not our own

This is no Programme, no Agenda – more a Way of Life. What the Conference members came away with was a desire to communicate this style of thinking and live in this sort of way. That is the point of this book. It is written in the hope that its content may be shared and pondered by others. If Christians of differing traditions who are willing to worship together, listen to each other, could use this book, it will have fulfilled its purpose. For we all seek the authority not of ourselves, but of our Crucified and Risen Lord. Stephen Sykes expressed this in his Sermon at the closing Eucharist and with this our book concludes.

POSTCRIPT:

Cleansing the Temple

A Sermon by Stephen Sykes

John 2.13–22:

After this he went down to Capernaum in company with his mother, his brothers, and his disciples, but they did not stay there long. As it was near the time of the Jewish Passover, Jesus went up to Jerusalem. There he found in the temple the dealers in cattle, sheep, and pigeons, and the money-changers seated at their tables. Jesus made a whip of cords and drove them out of the temple, sheep, cattle, and all. He upset the tables of the money-changers, scattering their coins. Then he turned on the dealers in pigeons: 'Take them out,' he said, 'you must not turn my Father's house into a market.' His disciples recalled the words of Scripture, 'Zeal for thy house will destroy me.' The Jews challenged Jesus: 'What sign', they asked, 'can you show as authority for your action?' 'Destroy this temple,' Jesus replied, 'and in three days I will raise it again.' They said, 'It has taken forty-six years to build this temple. Are you going to raise it again in three days?' But the temple he was speaking of was his body. After his resurrection his disciples recalled what he had said, and they believed the Scripture and the words that Jesus had spoken.

We may well thank God for the Church's Lectionary.

Here we are a curious collection of individuals, briefly bound together by a common interest; sociologically probably too homogeneous for our own good; psycho-

77

logically inclined to be interested in power and its exercise – which can't be normal; but otherwise normal in our suspicions, our desire to be loved, and in our capacity to be jolly and truculent by turns, to be mean-minded and generous in fits; in fact the usual Christian riff-raff, but riff-raff disconnected from its local context, an instant and rootless *koinonia*.

And if it had been left to us, or, more likely, a committee of us, to choose a Gospel for this weekend of reconciliation, would we have thought of the story of Jesus lashing the traders out of the Temple? We wouldn't, and then we would have missed the remarkable challenge – 'What sign can you show as authority for your action?'

Jesus' reply amounted to a riddle; the 'sign' was a sheer impossibility, a rebuilding programme to accelerate 46 years' construction work into three days. It must have a meaning – what meaning could it have? And here it is, says our author; Jesus was speaking of his body.

And why should the destruction and raising of his body be a sign of his authority? Because it is the pathway of his authority, the only pathway leading to the Cross.

> The Son of Man must be lifted up, as the serpent was lifted up by Moses in the wilderness (John 3.14)

The seat of authority for Jesus was to be the Cross, where his Kingship would be proclaimed in Hebrew, in Latin and in Greek, the languages of Scripture, Civil Administration and Philosophy.

> And the word of authority is the word of the Cross.

Now we know enough about ourselves to know what we may not do when we take this word for our own, as is our privilege.

We may not dramatize, by the Cross, our petty inconveniences; we may not fixate ourselves, by the Cross, upon failure; we may not indulge, by the Cross, whatever private leanings we have towards masochism.

For the word of the Cross is liberating. It liberates us precisely from the traders and the money-changers, from the nicely calculated less or more. The Cross is God's generosity, his love, his grace to sinners, who bring nothing in exchange except their sins. It is an exchange which brings exchanges to an end – there is no more trading to be done. The Temple is clear.

Do you not know that you are God's Temple, where the Spirit of the Lord dwells (I Cor. 3.16)?

Is it a measure of the degree to which we have lost sight of that generosity with which we are treated, when we grow used to the trading which goes on between Christians? Is this part of our Lord's 'No' to construing our relationships with each other on the basis of uncriticized political examples? Can we even begin to conceive that kind of friendship with each other which implies that we are debtors on a scale which makes trading ridiculous?

Perhaps here, where Jesus takes us apart with him for a little while, where the pressure of our immediate structures and compromises and failures is less intense, he can point us again to that Temple in which we are no longer dealers, but stones – in a riot of metaphor – 'living stones', initially perhaps roped together, but settling eventually into constructive and mutual interdependence, and built into a spiritual temple, a holy priesthood, offering spiritual sacrifices acceptable to God through Jesus Christ. (I Pet. 2.15)